OVERCOME SOCIAL ANXIETY AND SHYNESS

A Step-by-Step Self Help Action Plan to Overcome Social Anxiety, Defeat Shyness and Create Confidence

---

DR MATT LEWIS

DML

ISBN-10: 1548239658

ISBN-13: 978-1548239657

Contents

Part VI

Resources

About the Author

Dr Matt Lewis has a PhD in psychology and is a university academic delivering public and online courses in emotional well-being and personal development. He lectures in health psychology, exercise psychology, and mental health to undergraduate and postgraduate students. He also designs and delivers mindfulness, positive psychology, and Acceptance and Commitment Training (ACT) courses to the general public, trainers, teachers, and health professionals.

www.DrMattLewis.com

PART I
Safety Mode

UNDERSTANDING SOCIAL ANXIETY AND SHYNESS

ONE

Introduction

I first met Sarah at an anxiety workshop for university students in the Autumn of 2016. She was sitting at the back of the room, in the far right-hand corner, a large gap of empty chairs separating her from everyone else. I always attempt to make eye contact with everyone in the room during my workshops, but whenever I looked in her direction her head would bow and I couldn't catch her eye. During the group exercises, she stayed in her seat rather than joining in with the others, preferring to take notes or stare at her phone.

After the workshop had finished and I'd answered students' questions, she was still sitting in her seat in the corner, so I walked over and introduced myself. She looked up at me, her face and neck flushed, and told me her name in a whispered voice. I asked her why she had come to the workshop as gently as I could, and after a few tears, her story came flooding out.

Sarah's social anxiety was so debilitating that she didn't attend her classes on the first day of university, knowing it was possible that the lecturer would ask students to go around the room and introduce themselves. Just sitting in a room, waiting to introduce herself to strangers who will stare at her, makes her feel physically sick. She's aware that her voice sounds shaky and her face reddens when speaking in public. Sarah knew she wouldn't have been able to think clearly because her anxiety in those situations is often intense, and she might have made a "stupid mistake." She once even blanked on her own name.

So she skipped the first day of classes and then got scared about being the only new student in the next set of classes. It spiralled out of control, and she didn't attend any lectures during the first three weeks of university. Sarah was informed that if she didn't attend within the first four weeks, she would have to leave the course, so she booked an appointment with her doctor to discuss her anxiety. As the first available appointment was two weeks away, on the advice of the course administrator, she had signed up for my workshop. So here she was. She said, *"It just feels impossible to beat."*

As a lecturer, I often hear stories from students about how anxiety has impacted their academic work and, usually, their lives outside of university, too. Answering questions in lectures was terrifying for many, and participating in group work and class discussions often caused sleepless nights. Then there was the dreaded class presentation; the majority of students feared them, and many even excused themselves from them with medical notes referring to severe anxiety.

Having suffered from anxiety myself, I empathised and understood many of their fears and struggles. I could also provide them with the powerful hope that it's possible to change your relationship with anxiety and manage it in a way that not only helps you to survive at university but enables you to thrive while still living by your core values and being true to yourself. I could explain how someone like me, scared of speaking on the phone and terrified of social gatherings, could now lecture in front of more than 200 students.

In cases of severe anxiety, I always advised students to seek help from the university support services or their General Practitioner. I also discussed strategies that could help them with their anxiety and get their coursework back on track. As more and more students approached me, I worked on a guide to help with everyday anxiety that students could take away with them after their appointments. I designed the guide to be preventative — to stop early symptoms from developing into clinical problems — but also to go beyond that, to build confidence and help them become unstuck and move forward with everything they needed to do to pass the course and get on with their lives.

Students who didn't suffer from anxiety but had heard the exercises helped build more confident and positive lives approached me and asked for access to the guide. The guide developed into an online course and a book on overcoming general anxiety.[1] Following the book's publication and related public workshops, I received many requests for more specific help with social anxiety. So, I set to work on a new book that tailored the information and exercises to help those for whom social anxiety was a particular problem. You're reading that book right now. It's based on the same principles as the previous book but focuses on applying them to social situations that provoke anxiety.

Although my background is working with students, the approach used in this book isn't age or student-specific. It includes background information on how social anxiety can develop in people of all ages, alongside preventative and interventional exercises derived from a breadth of research on managing social anxiety and shyness and building confidence. I've used these exercises in workshops for those experiencing social anxiety in colleges, the workplace, and everyday life.

The approach uses evidence-based exercises from mindfulness, Acceptance and Commitment Therapy (ACT), and positive psychology. Social anxiety can paralyse us, and sometimes, dealing with the briefest of social interactions can seem insurmountable, so the information is reduced into small chunks, with brief chapters that can be digested easily and quickly. With a workbook format, the book is a toolkit for overcoming social anxiety and also provides practical help for calming and reducing panic attacks.

The book starts with some background information explaining why and how social anxiety develops and then highlights the evidence on which the book's main principles are built. Although it may be tempting to skip these parts, understanding your social anxiety and being convinced by evidence that the exercises work should help bring change to your life more quickly and increase your motivation to apply the practices. The theory section is concise and won't take long to read. However, you can start with the practical exercises if you want to get started right away.

There are four main steps in this revolutionary approach, and I've seen it change people's lives time and time again. You're going to learn to:

1. Understand how social anxiety and shyness develop.
2. Build a solid foundation for behaviour change.
3. Effectively manage anxious thoughts and feelings.
4. Be confident in social situations.

The principles and practices you will learn in the book go beyond managing social anxiety. They will also help you become unstuck, build confidence and start living. Overcoming social anxiety isn't easy, but it is possible with courage and commitment.

Throughout the book, you will be asked to do things that make you feel uncomfortable, but discomfort is the price of admission to a meaningful life. The exercises will walk you through these difficult actions step-by-step, allowing you to develop courage. Courage is not the absence of fear; courage is fear walking.

Using the latest scientific and academic research, you will be able to:

- Learn how living in 'safety mode' can diminish your life.
- Create a mindset that will allow you to believe change is possible.
- Build the foundations for a calm and peaceful mind.
- Avoid mental exhaustion and increase energy.
- Effectively handle anxious thoughts and feelings as they arise.
- Tame the voice in your head and reduce anxiety in social situations.
- Become unstuck and able to take action in situations you would typically avoid.
- Build confidence in both small and large social situations.
- Take steps to create a fulfilling and meaningful life.

The book contains:

- Step-by-step practical exercises.
- Access to audio exercises and online resources.
- A social anxiety action plan to help apply all the learned skills.

This book will be helpful for those who struggle with:

- General Anxiety
- Social Anxiety
- Shyness
- Anxiety Disorder
- Panic Attacks
- Panic Disorder
- Agoraphobia

∿

I introduced Sarah to skills and exercises that gradually changed her mindset about her social anxiety. With support from her friends and family and a lot of courage, she successfully completed her degree at university.

~

HOW TO USE THIS BOOK

I wrote this book to be read easily and quickly, with the intention that you can begin to understand your social anxiety and apply the practical exercises as quickly. I recommend you first read the book in its entirety and practise the exercises along the way. This should give you a feel of what works best for you. It is worth keeping in mind that some practices may take time to reveal their full potential. This is why they are called practices. While you will see some immediate positive changes after many exercises, others will take a little more time before they reveal their true power.

Many exercises don't require huge changes; they are small nudges that will push you in a more peaceful and confident direction, making a positive long-term impact on your social anxiety. While you may think it would be best to make significant changes quickly, you'll find that change is more successful at a calm and steady pace. Think tortoise, not hare. Doing too much too soon is sometimes problematic and overwhelming and can cause discouragement.

Self-help books often discuss change in terms of grand goals and complete transformation in a short period of time, but research points to the opposite being more effective—small conscious tweaks that are aligned with personal meaning and values. These small everyday changes can make a huge difference over time and become far more powerful than attempts to make massive changes over short periods.

This book is practical and effective. Methods that promise instant and magical transformations lose their impact when we have to leave our comfort zone and the fairy dust blows away. The benefits of doing the exercises will build over time. Soon, you will find your relationship with social anxiety changing for the better, along with a growing sense of peace and the courage to tackle social situations and interactions you previously avoided.

FINDING OUT WHAT WORKS BEST

The exercises included in the book have been tested and scientifically validated on various populations. I've included references and links to these studies where applicable. However, there is no such thing as an 'average person'; you may find that some exercises work better than others. Only by applying these exercises in the real world will you determine which ones are most effective for you. Test out the exercises for yourself and see what works best. When something works well, use an evolutionary-style approach and consider how you can change it further so it fits in with your values and lifestyle in a way that makes it even more effective. Don't be afraid of testing different approaches out, and don't worry if, after giving it some time, an exercise doesn't work well for you – see it as part of the process of finding out what does.

The book is divided into five main parts:

1. Safety Mode: Understanding Social Anxiety and Shyness. In this part, we'll discover what 'safety mode' is, how it can diminish our lives, and what we can do to break free from it. We will also explain how and why social anxiety and shyness develop, what it feels like, when it can be helpful, and when it becomes a problem. We will outline the two different pathways to anxiety and discover why some popular anxiety treatments will fail, as they only consider one of these pathways.

2. Preparing to Change: Building a Solid Foundation for Behaviour Transformation. This will be the start of the practical journey. It's about considering and understanding who you are, assessing how balanced your life is, and preparing you to make changes. We'll also introduce exercises to create a solid foundation by calming the mind, increasing energy, and preparing you for the mindfulness skills introduced in the next section.

3. Three Key Skills: Dealing with Anxious Thoughts and Feelings. Having built a foundation, we will now look at strategies that will help you change your relationship with anxiety and allow you to manage uncomfortable thoughts and feelings as they arise. Understanding how your thoughts and feelings work can create a calmer, clearer mind when interacting with others. This part will introduce you to three essential skills from Acceptance and Commitment Therapy: defusion, expansion, and engagement. Applying these skills will help you effectively deal with anxiety that occurs both before and during social situations.

4. Action Mode: A Step-By-Step Social Anxiety Action Plan. The dress rehearsal is over; it's time to use the skills you've learned in the real world. Social anxiety often leaves us feeling stuck and unable to take action. We don't do the things we would like to do and avoid taking action on many of the things we need to do, often making difficult situations even worse. In this part, you'll learn a step-by-step process that allows you to expose yourself safely to the social situations you most fear. You will also learn how to weave the practices into everyday life in a way that becomes sustainable over the long term. Life begins at the end of your comfort zone, and we will leave it here.

5. Emergency Exercises: Managing Fight, Flight, or Freeze. Anxiety can sometimes feel so overpowering that we either panic or freeze, so this part contains short and simple exercises that focus on reducing the extreme symptoms of anxiety. It includes exercises that can be practised when feeling particularly anxious, stressed, or at the edge of losing it. We will also outline what can be done to reduce the effects of panic attacks and how to eliminate future episodes.

TWO

Understanding Social Anxiety

I'm staring at the phone, willing myself to pick it up and dial the number. I've been trying to build the courage to do this for five minutes. I need to make a dental appointment for my annual check-up, but I know I should have made the appointment over three months ago.

The dental practice has a habit of striking off patients who don't visit for check-ups at least once a year, and it's been at least fifteen months since my last appointment. *"They'll be angry and dismissive of me"*, I think. I look at the time - it's 9:30 am – it feels like I'm calling at the wrong time; early morning is a busy period for the overworked receptionists. That will make the situation even worse. I'm afraid of talking to an unknown person, worried I'll be 'putting them out' and making them upset with me.

My heart is beating rapidly, and my mouth feels dry. I speak out loud to check how my voice sounds. It's a little shaky. *'Come on, Matt, it's only a phone call,"* I think, *"one of dozens they receive every day."* I pick up the phone and rapidly punch in the number. The line rings, and I end the call before it's answered. I'll try later. Yes, later. After lunchtime will be better, when it's less busy and I feel more confident. I'll call from my office at work.

The time spent deliberating over the phone call has left me

running late for work. I must get a move on. I leave the house to walk to the train station. I reach the high street, and I'm aware of people waiting at the bus stop opposite, looking in my direction. I feel self-conscious; it's as if they are staring at me. My gait feels strange; walking doesn't seem natural; my legs feel heavy, weak, and out of sync. I must look weird. I see my reflection in a shop window. I definitely look weird.

I decide to leave the road at the next turning and take the quieter route to the station even though it will take longer and I'm already running late. I miss my train. I'm annoyed, angry, and disappointed with myself.

THE COMPONENTS OF ANXIETY

The events above illustrate the main components of anxiety and the two different routes that lead to it. Anxiety can be created from two different areas of the brain: the cortex, which creates anxiety based on what we think about, and the amygdala, which reacts to what is happening in our environment. Remember these two routes because they are vital in managing our anxiety, and we'll discuss them in detail in Chapter 5.

However, it would be beneficial to start with the components of anxiety. If we know what our anxiety is made up of, we can reflect on what is going on inside us, make sense of our experiences, and then manage it more effectively.

Researchers and clinicians have identified three basic components of anxiety:

1. Physiological

The first of these components is physiological arousal. This happens when our fight, flight or freeze reaction kicks in and adrenaline starts pumping, producing a cascade of physiological symptoms.

These symptoms may include shortness of breath, muscle

tension, sweating, dizziness or lightheadedness, stomach upset, tremors and twitches, headaches, and frequent urination or diarrhoea. Physiological arousal can be helpful when we're in a genuinely dangerous or challenging situation, but it can also be detrimental to our physical and mental health when we respond frequently to non-life-threatening situations in this way.

2. Cognitive and Emotional

The second component is the cognitive and emotional part of anxiety. This is future-orientated thinking, fear, and accurate and inaccurate risk appraisal. So it's ruminating about what could go wrong and how awful that will feel. It's not that all future-orientated thinking is bad – it's essential for us to think about the future and plan for what may go wrong - this is what makes us such a successful species – however, it can often be inaccurate and unhelpful.

3. Behavioural

The final essential component is the behavioural aspect of anxiety – the avoidance behaviour and rituals – in essence, the things we do in order not to feel anxious. We may avoid the anxious situation or task altogether or distract ourselves from it with alcohol, eating, social media, or several other behaviours.

Understandably, we try to avoid anxiety because we find it very unpleasant. However, in avoiding anxiety, we often restrict our lives or end up causing ourselves more problems. We can sometimes, with the right mindset, respond to anxiety in a positive way, such as doing extra preparation if we feel anxious about an interview or a test, but often we respond in an unhelpful way.

Before reading further, I'd like you to complete a quick exercise that will only take a few minutes.

∾

Exercise: Recognising the Components of Anxiety

Step 1: Take a moment to think of a social situation that makes you feel moderately anxious. Something real, not imagined. Maybe it's a person you feel nervous around, a social situation you often try to avoid, or an up-and-coming social event that provokes some anxiety. Imagine you have to meet that person right now, go to that social situation right now, or involve yourself in that social event right now. Take a minute to do this.

Step 2: Now, see if you can be aware of and identify those three basic components of anxiety.

- Firstly, is there a physiological response? Maybe your breathing has changed, your heart is beating faster, your stomach has butterflies, or your muscles have become a little tense.
- Secondly, is there a cognitive or emotional response? Some future-orientated thinking, a scene of what could happen in the future? A feeling of fear?
- Finally, is there a behavioural aspect to it? Are you thinking of ways to avoid it, put it off, or distract yourself from it?

That is all you need to do for now: be aware of the components. Later in the book, we'll talk about how to deal with these components and manage anxiety effectively, but it's vital that we learn to notice it and become mindful of what is happening rather than falling into automatic pilot. Over the following days, see if you can notice when you're feeling anxious, and when you are aware, try to identify the three components.

WHERE DOES MY ANXIETY COME FROM?

While knowing the reasons why we are anxious may not be enough to alleviate our anxiety, self-awareness of where our anxiety comes from and how it is triggered can be a key first step. Finding the cause of our anxiety can be difficult as many possible variables contribute to the way we feel, and they vary from individual to individual. Let's look at some of the most common reasons.

Our Brains Evolved to be Anxious: For our early ancestors to survive in dangerous environments, their brains evolved to help keep them safe by being very attentive to threats. Consequently, they remembered every bad thing that happened and spent much of their lives anticipating more trouble, and this is the mind we inherited from them. Despite living in relatively safe environments in the modern world, these instincts can still set us up for a number of difficulties. We'll explore these difficulties in more detail in *Chapter 4: Our Anxious Brains.*

Family Genes: The genes we inherit from our grandparents and parents may play a role, but only by creating a disposition towards anxiety. Our environment, experiences, and lifestyle will determine whether we 'switch on' our propensity for anxiety, so we play a significant role in determining our personal experience of it.[2]

Life Events: Major life events, both good and bad, often affect our anxiety levels. A death in the family, the end of a relationship, being involved in an accident, or losing a job. Experiences like this make us fearful and uncertain about life. After such events, life can seem unstable, and anxiety can kick in to protect us from similar things happening in the future. If we withdraw, we can't get hurt. An accumulation of small but stressful life events, such as arguments with family members, difficult periods at work, and financial hardship, can also contribute to our anxiety in the long term.

Childhood Experiences: How we were raised considerably influences our mindset, thinking styles, and emotional coping strategies. We often learn how to react to difficult situations by modelling our parents or guardians and listening to their opinions about who we are, how we should feel, and how we should handle life. These influences can shape our expectations and how we perceive ourselves, others, and the world, particularly how we cope with stress and difficult challenges.

Lifestyle: Not taking care of ourselves or continually putting the needs of others before our own can create anxiety or make an anxiety problem worse. The impact of lifestyle factors is often ignored as people search for a magic bullet to overcome their anxiety. We will address these lifestyle components in more detail in *Chapter 9: Avoiding Exhaustion and Increasing Energy.*

Health Problems: Chronic health problems can make us anxious about the present and future, particularly if we're in pain or think the issues are beyond our control.

Alcohol / Drugs: People may drink alcohol or take drugs (including prescribed medication) to mask anxiety or block its effects. While this may give us some short-term relief, it tends to make our anxiety worse in the long run while also creating other complications.

This list only contains some of the most common causes, so don't worry if you don't recognise any of these in your experience of anxiety. Wherever your anxiety has originated from, it is still possible to overcome it. Change is achievable.

GENERAL ANXIETY, SOCIAL ANXIETY, AND SHYNESS

We started the chapter with some examples of social anxiety - anxiety that is linked explicitly to social situations. **General anxiety** differs from social anxiety in that it isn't confined just to one aspect of our lives but involves anxiety across wide-ranging areas, from personal health to work performance to the state of the world.

If you struggle with **social anxiety**, it's likely that you will also have moderately high levels of general anxiety, but the social anxiety aspect is the most troubling. More often than not, anxiety cannot be neatly compartmentalised into different types but over-laps into many areas.

How does social anxiety differ from shyness if it is specifically linked to social situations? Although both have much in common, there is a small but distinct difference between them.

Shyness refers to the tendency to feel nervous or timid when interacting with others, especially strangers. Talking or engaging with people outside your usual social circle can be frightening, and you might find yourself avoiding these situations as much as possible.

Social anxiety includes the feelings and behaviours of shyness but expands beyond this to also experiencing anxiety when being observed by others (for example, when walking outside) and performing in front of others (for example, giving a presentation).

So, while shyness only involves fear of engaging with others, social anxiety is about fear and nervousness around interacting with others, being observed by others, and performing in front of others.

Socially anxious people fear these types of situations because of what they believe might happen. Their anxiety about what might happen usually falls into one or more of the following categories:

1. Fear of saying or doing something embarrassing (such as stumbling over their words).
2. Fear of displaying symptoms of their anxiety (quivering voice, shaking, blushing).
3. Fear of being judged critically by others (seen as boring, stupid, unattractive).

The specific details of the situations that cause anxiety will vary from person to person; some people are just a little shy with strangers, while others are intensely shy with almost everyone they encounter. Some people fear a specific type of social situation (such as giving speeches), while others are anxious in most social situations.

This doesn't mean we should always aim to be socially engaged. There's nothing wrong with wanting to take a quiet route when walking, avoiding people we don't want to speak to, or turning down an unnecessary speaking engagement. However, when social anxiety significantly interferes with our lives, stops us from pursuing the things we would like to do, or causes us to avoid doing the things we need to do in everyday life, it's time to address the problem and take action.

Now, let's examine more closely how we tend to behave when anxious about social situations and why living in 'Safety Mode' can limit our lives and cause further problems.

THREE

Safety Mode

When we avoid social situations in order to escape anxiety, we are entering into what psychologists refer to as 'safety mode'. While keeping us safe and out of the way of social danger, safety mode comes at a cost.

PLAYING SAFE

If, like me, when walking, you've ever taken a longer, more inconvenient route to avoid other people, stuck to a close friend all night at a party, or turned down a speaking engagement that would further your career, you've been operating in safety mode.

The goal of safety mode is to protect us from the feared outcomes we discussed in the last chapter: embarrassing ourselves, displaying symptoms of our anxiety, or being judged negatively by others. These outcomes are collectively known as **'social danger'**, and those with social anxiety try to avoid social danger at all costs.

Four individual components contribute to safety mode:

1. Intense focus on social danger.
2. Engaging in safety behaviours.

3. Fusing with anxious thoughts.
4. Resisting anxious feelings.

Let's go through these components step-by-step to understand how they influence our behaviour and keep us stuck in safety mode.

1. Intense Focus on Social Danger

Those with social anxiety tend to focus on the signs of social danger when thinking about a social situation. Rather than considering all aspects of the situation, we focus our attention on how we could embarrass ourselves or make a bad impression. For example, we may focus on possible visible signs of anxiety (trembling hands, shaky voice, etc.); what we could say that would make us look stupid, boring, or inadequate (getting someone's name wrong, being unable to contribute to a conversation); or what we might physically do to make ourselves look awkward or incompetent (walking strangely, tripping, spilling a drink etc.).

The more we focus on ourselves in this way, the more the anxious feelings intensify. This original focus on social danger also puts us on 'high alert' for other signs of social danger, such as the way people look at us as we're walking by (*Is that person smirking at me?*) or the reactions of others as we speak (*She looks bored.*).

2. Engaging in Safety Behaviours

Safety behaviours are the actions we take to protect ourselves from social danger. While they make us feel safe and help us to avoid feeling anxious, they often come at a cost. Safety behaviours are divided into two main categories: **avoidance behaviours** and **hiding behaviours**.

i) Avoidance Behaviours

Avoidance behaviours involve staying away from social situations that make us anxious. So we may avoid a party we are invited to by turning down the invitation or excusing ourselves by pretending we're ill. We don't apply for a promotion that involves making a presentation. We don't approach someone to ask for directions even though we're lost and running late.

If we avoid social situations that give us anxiety, we can't mess up, do something embarrassing, or be seen as an inconvenience. However, although these avoidance actions may make us feel safe, with each party invitation we turn down, job we don't apply for, and conversation we avoid, our lives become a little more restricted. Life can become small and unlived.

Avoiding anxiety-inducing situations can also backfire and bring about the very outcome we fear. For example, if we keep on turning down social situations for fear of disappointing people, others may interpret this as us being aloof or unfriendly and feel let down by or disappointed with our behaviour.

This is not to say that we should always embrace every social situation; it's okay to turn down or avoid social situations that we aren't interested in or don't want to attend. However, we shouldn't restrict our lives by avoiding social situations that we want to participate in or would benefit from.

Safety Mode Exercise 1 - The Costs of Avoidance

A printable template of this exercise can also be found online using the link below. Just type the exact link into your web browser to access the template: http://bit.ly/2rqEg25

This quick exercise will help raise awareness of your avoidance behaviours and the associated costs they bring to your life. We

can repeat avoidance behaviours so often that they become automatic, so it's essential to make ourselves aware of them and their
potential impact on our lives.

Spend five minutes to think carefully through the last few
months of your life and come up with as many situations that you
can remember purposely avoiding. Also, consider the potential
costs of doing so. Remember, the social situations may or may not
be unique to you, and they don't have to fit into a stereotype of
social anxiety.

Situations Avoided	Costs

∾

ii) Hiding Behaviours

We aren't able to avoid all social situations that make us anxious
or don't always consider we need to. Instead, we sometimes use
behaviours designed to minimise our anxious symptoms and try
to control the impression that we are making. These are **hiding
behaviours** and can vary from individual to individual,
depending on what we are specifically anxious about and the type
of social situations we can find ourselves in. Examples of hiding
behaviours include:

- **Public situations**: Pretending to be on the phone or always wearing headphones when outside.
- **Anxiety symptoms**: Covering up with make-up, hats, sunglasses or other clothing to hide physical symptoms such as blushing or trembling.
- **Eating out**: Ordering the same food as others at a restaurant to avoid choosing the 'wrong' thing or not sending back food that isn't cooked correctly.
- **Meeting people**: Always being agreeable and pleasant and hiding your opinions to prevent people from being upset with you.
- **Public speaking**: Reading speeches quickly and word for word or getting someone else to do it for you.
- **Social gatherings**: Avoid conversations by sticking to a 'safe' person, only talking to 'safe' people, or engaging in helping activities in the kitchen to avoid conversations.
- **Personal attention**: Arriving early at meetings or gatherings and sitting at the back to avoid drawing attention to yourself. Exercising at inconvenient times to avoid contact with others and ensure no one observes you.

This is not an exhaustive list. People engage in many individual hiding behaviours. We'll have a closer look at these in the next exercise.

While these hiding behaviours aren't as limiting and costly as avoidance - after all, they allow us to be present in social situations - they can still be costly in a number of ways.

Hiding behaviours often require a lot of effort and can be time-consuming. We can be so focused on keeping safe that we aren't fully present, missing out on the richness many social situations can offer our lives. These behaviours can make it challenging to meet new people, share our opinions, and participate in activities we would benefit from.

Using hiding behaviours can also become a vicious circle. If a social situation goes reasonably well when we're using hiding behaviours, we will be more likely to use them again, bringing about the belief that they are always required for us to survive social situations. So we continue to use them and miss out, with our world getting smaller and smaller. In the next exercise, we will focus on uncovering your hiding behaviours and the possible costs to your life.

Safety Mode Exercise 2 - The Costs of Hiding Behaviours

A printable template of this exercise can also be found online using the link below. Just type the exact link into your web browser to access the template: http://bit.ly/2rZUK4F

Social Situation	Hiding Behaviours	Costs
e.g. Walking in public places	I often drive short distances instead walking. I sometimes wear headphones or pretend to be talking on my phone	I get less fresh air, exercise and spend more money on fuel and parking. I don't get to interact with other people, or take in the sights and sounds around me.
1.		
2.		
3.		

Using the table above, list social situations that make you feel anxious in the lefthand column, the hiding behaviours you usually use in the middle column, and the costs of using those behaviours in the righthand column.

3. Fusing with Anxious Thoughts

In safety mode, we also tend to 'fuse' with our anxious thoughts. We're considered to be fusing with thoughts when we get caught up in them, give them all our attention, and see them as the absolute truth. So when we're contemplating a future social situation, we may have thoughts such as, "*They're going to think I'm an idiot if I try to talk to them, better just not say anything.*" or "*They're not interested in talking to me, I sound so boring.*" We focus all our attention on these thoughts and get caught up in them.

These thoughts then push us into using safety behaviours such as keeping quiet or focusing on our phones instead of interacting with others. When we fuse with our thoughts and engage in safety behaviours, we can feel upset or annoyed with ourselves later and regret that we haven't met any new people or contributed to conversations - the costs of trying to keep safe.

We can also fuse with our thoughts during a social situation. We may be unable to concentrate on a conversation as we focus on unhelpful thoughts such as "*My voice sounds shaky, I must sound really nervous.*" or "*I must be boring them. I can't think of anything interesting to say.*" When we get caught up in our thoughts like this, we are disconnected from what is happening right in front of us, making engaging with our environment difficult. Our anxious thoughts become our reality and dominate our behaviour.

4. Resisting Anxious Feelings

When thinking about future social situations or directly involved in a social interaction, we also tend to focus on our anxious feelings. That is the emotional aspect (the feeling of fear) and the physical sensations that go along with it (rapidly beating heart, sweating, shaking). We often try to resist or push away these uncomfortable emotions, feelings, or sensations. So when we realise that our stomach feels tense, our voice sounds shaky, or our forehead is sweating, we resist rather than accept we feel this way and continue to focus on the present moment. We attempt to avoid an interaction, leave a situation, or focus on pushing away our feelings rather than focus on what is happening in front of us.

MOVING FROM SAFETY MODE TO ACTION MODE

Later in the book, we will focus on dealing with these anxious thoughts and feelings and taking action, learning how to move from safety mode into action mode. However, before we do this, it would be beneficial to understand why we have evolved to experience anxiety when we find it so painful and troublesome. What is its purpose in our lives? To understand the role of anxiety, we need to take a journey into our past.

FOUR

Our Anxious Brains

While modern life can intensify our anxiety, the building blocks for our struggle with social anxiety can be found way back in the past with some of our earliest descendants. There was only one goal for our early ancestors – survival – and we developed to survive above everything else. Being happy wasn't a consideration to the evolutionary forces that shaped our early behaviours; the main aim was for us to survive long enough to mate and reproduce. Life beyond survival and reproduction didn't matter.

However, the instincts and intellectual abilities that helped us to survive in the past—and can still serve us well now—have also created negative consequences for us as individuals today. We didn't evolve to be happy; we evolved to survive. This has set us up for many difficulties. Why is this?

Well, imagine what life was like for our very early descendants, the hominids. They were much slower than most other animals alive then; in comparison, they had average sight and smell and weren't relatively big or strong.

To survive, our ancestors had to have other advantages. These came in the form of an opposable thumb and flexible fingers—that could make tools and weapons—and also, in the brain, a growing cerebral cortex. The cortex played a vital role in the survival of hominids by remembering moments of pleasure and pain. It did this in order to figure out how to maximise future pleasure and avoid future pain. This motivated our ancestors to survive while also keeping them safe.

The cortex produces thoughts tailored to the demands of its environment, and the environment of our early descendants was quite different from the modern developed world we now live in. Our ancestors lived in small bands or groups, and it was rare for them to meet new people, and it was often dangerous when they did. Social situations outside of their small group were to be avoided or escaped from. Strangers were dangerous.

It wasn't just unexpected social situations that put them in danger. They also faced starvation, parasites, illness, injury, and the hazards of childbirth, and there were no medications, painkillers, medical facilities, or police to help them. This was where the human brain developed, and it was a hazardous and threatening habitat.

In this dangerous environment, our ancestors could make two possible types of mistakes when encountering strangers. They could flee, thinking they were hostile, when in fact they were friendly, or they could wait to greet them, thinking they were friendly, when in fact they were hostile. The cost of the first mistake was needless anxiety, while the price of the second mistake was death. So, we evolved to make the first type of mistake multiple times to avoid making the second mistake even once.

There may have been some happy hominids who were care-free and not continually focused on looking out for danger, but, likely, they weren't the ones who reproduced our ancestors. Their genes wouldn't have survived. They would have died before they could reproduce. So our ancestors remembered every bad thing that happened and spent much of their lives antici-pating more trouble, and this is the mind we inherited from them.

INTERACTION OF SURVIVAL SYSTEMS

Along with the cerebral cortex, several inbuilt survival systems help to keep us safe from danger and motivated to survive. However, how these systems interact can sometimes cause us to feel anxious, stressed, and unhappy.

1. The Negativity Bias

Research has discovered we developed a 'negativity bias'.[3] So, if you had ten good social encounters today but had one negative experience, it's more likely that you'll remember the one negative social encounter when you go to bed tonight. This is the negativity bias in practice. How and why does this happen?

Well, there's a part of the brain shaped like an almond called the amygdala, designed to evaluate our environmental circumstances and decide whether something is a threat or not. The amygdala reacts far more rapidly and thoroughly to negative than positive stimuli. As a result, the negative contaminates the positive far more easily than the positive contaminates the negative. This is why we react more strongly to threats than positive events, why trust is easy to lose but difficult to gain, why negative political campaigns dominate the media, and why we spend more time on social media criticising what we don't like rather than promoting what we love. Negativity gets people's attention more quickly and easily and takes precedence over positive information.

The negativity bias developed in harsh conditions but continues in today's relatively safe environments. Thus, we can react to comparatively safe and benign conditions, such as talking to a stranger, going on a date, or making a speech, as though they are life-or-death situations, and often, we expect the worst.

2. The Emergency Arousal System

The negativity bias also interacts with our emergency arousal system—**the fight, flight, or freeze response**—which can be triggered by our negative thoughts. When triggered, the amygdala, from its central position in the brain, sends instructions to energise the sympathetic nervous system, increasing the levels of hormones such as adrenaline and cortisol in the bloodstream.

This results in a number of changes in the body, including elevated heart rate, rapid breathing, dilated pupils, blood flow diverted away from the digestive tract to the limbs, and tensed muscles. The body is now primed for action. When this happens, you may feel like your heart is pounding, your body is trembling, and your stomach and bowels are distressed.

It's highly beneficial when this reaction is needed — such as in a life-saving emergency or challenging environment. However, if the arousal system overreacts, it can set off a fully blown panic attack when no logical reason for fear exists. Our bodies evolved to react like this occasionally (like when we see a dangerous animal or need to run away from a group of enemies). We don't cope very well when it's activated all day, over weeks, months, or years. When it is, it sets us up for many anxiety-related ailments, both physical and mental.

Indeed, long-term elevated cortisol levels can lower immune function and bone density, elevate blood pressure, cholesterol and body weight, increase the risk of heart disease, depression and mental illness, and interfere with learning and memory.[4] Later in the book, when discussing mindset, we will consider how changing how we think about our stress response can minimise these negative effects and even benefit our health. However, the stress response didn't evolve to be continually activated for long periods, but only when needed for survival or to help us in a challenging situation.

3. Seeking Out Pleasure and Avoiding Pain

Also, as mentioned earlier, we evolved to pursue pleasure and avoid pain. This motivates us to do things that perpetuate our DNA, usually through pleasurable experiences such as sex, friendship, eating, sleeping, and finding a safe home. As a result, we can get hooked on constantly seeking these things, and when we don't have the perfect conditions to experience them or fear we could lose them, it makes us feel distressed. So we're not only impacted by immediate threats to our survival but also the fear we won't get what we evolved to seek out or we may lose what we already have.

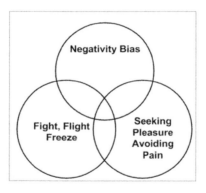

So these three survival systems do an excellent job of keeping us alive while also pushing us to experience pleasure, but their interactions also prime us for anxiety.

NEUROPLASTICITY

On top of these three hardwired survival systems, we have also discovered learning changes the brain through what neurologists call experience-dependent neuroplasticity. Scientists used to think the brain reached maturity around the age of 25 years and then deteriorated. Now we know it's much more like a muscle, and while it ultimately weakens over our lifespan, when we use specific neural pathways in our brain, they become stronger, and when we don't, they become weaker.[5]

The principle of neuroplasticity is relatively simple: information travels throughout the brain via electrical impulses that move along nerve cells called neurons. For an impulse to travel from one neuron to another it has to pass through synapses separated by a space called the synaptic cleft. Whenever we have a thought, a synapse fires a chemical across the cleft to another synapse, building a bridge over which the electric signal can cross, carrying the information along its charge. Every time this chemical is fired, the synapses grow closer together in order to decrease the distance the electrical impulse has to cross.

This is the brain rewiring its circuitry, physically changing itself, to make it easier and more likely the most used synapses will share the chemical link and fire together. This makes it easier for the information to be passed on. So, the repetition of signals travelling down the same pathways, through repeated behaviour and learning, reshapes the brain. This is why, in 1949, neuroscientist Carla Shatz coined the term *'Neurons that fire together, wire together'*. As a result, negative (and positive) thought patterns can deepen and become more habitual, like a river bed that deepens over time.

With all of these evolutionarily hardwired systems operating to help us survive, it's no wonder we often find life difficult in the modern world. Later in the book, we will look at interventions developed in response to this complex evolutionary predicament. The interventions are far-reaching in their effect on mental well-being because they address two challenges simultaneously:

- Firstly, they can provide insight into the patterns of the mind that create anxiety and suffering, radically changing our views of ourselves and others.

- Secondly, they can retrain the brain not to respond automatically using these instinctual patterns.

Now we have some understanding of why anxiety developed, how it has played a vital role in helping us survive, and why we can find it so troublesome, we will next take a closer look at the processes that take place in the brain when we experience anxiety. Understanding where the anxiety response starts is critical to effectively managing our anxious brains.

FIVE

The Two Routes to Anxiety

I n this chapter, we will dive into the anatomy of anxiety. We'll explain where anxiety originates and how it travels throughout the brain. I've tried to make this chapter easy to read but didn't want to leave out crucial details, so don't worry if it takes a little while for you to grasp some of the processes. Hang on in there. Understanding the brain structures involved can help us to work out how best to manage our anxious thoughts and feelings in social situations.

At the beginning of the second chapter, we mentioned that anxiety can originate from two different areas of the brain. Anxiety produced as a result of our thoughts is initiated in the **cortex**, and anxiety produced by our reaction to what is happening in our environment is initiated in the **amygdala**.

From this point on, I'll refer to anxiety originating in the cortex as the **'thought route'** and anxiety originating in the amygdala as the **'reactive route'**. Everyone is capable of experiencing anxiety through both routes, but it's important to recognise which route the anxiety has originated from to manage it effectively.

We'll now summarise how each of the routes works and how we can best manage the anxiety that originates in each one. If you want to read about the routes in greater detail, I recommend the book *Rewire Your Anxious Brain* by Catherine Pittman.

In the personal examples I gave at the beginning of the book, anxiety was aroused in the thought route by my thoughts about how the receptionist at the dental surgery would react to my phone call. The anxiety produced by people looking at me as I walked past the bus stop was a result of my amygdala reacting to the environment – the reactive route. Knowing the differences between the two routes enables us to design practical interventions and exercises that effectively change our experience of social anxiety and modify the circuits in the brain to help us regulate it successfully.

Over the last twenty years, neurological research has revolutionised our knowledge of the brain structures and circuits involved in producing anxiety. Most current treatments for anxiety, such as psychotherapy or Cognitive Behavioural Therapy (CBT), are based on changing and disputing thoughts and, therefore, target cortex-based anxiety, often only impacting the thought route.

While they can be very effective for managing anxious thoughts, using these exercises when experiencing reactive amygdala-based anxiety is often ineffectual and can sometimes be detrimental. Let's look at the two routes in more detail.

1. THE REACTIVE ROUTE

The amygdala is located centrally in the brain and is involved in both routes to anxiety. Like a built-in security system, it scans the environment for any sign of danger, getting its sensory information (sights, sounds, smells, touch) from another structure in the brain called the thalamus. The thalamus sends the sensory information to the cortex and the amygdala, but crucially, the amygdala receives this information first (see the following diagram).

This is because the amygdala is wired to respond rapidly to save your life; it's an evolution-based safety measure. If the amygdala recognises the information received as dangerous, it immediately triggers the emergency arousal system: the fight, flight, or freeze response.

The arousal response energises the sympathetic nervous system, which produces a rapid cascade of physiological arousal, resulting in several changes in the body to ensure we are primed for action. This means your amygdala can react to protect you from danger before your cortex is even aware of the threat. This is why we can respond by jumping out of the way of a speeding car or rapidly pulling back our hand when it touches a hot surface before we have time to understand what we're reacting to.

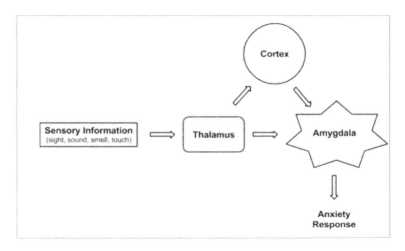

It takes a little more time for the cortex to receive this information and for us to understand what is happening. So we may quickly jump away from a tomato stem that looks like a spider but recover almost immediately when the information reaches the cortex, is assessed, and is recognised as a harmless tomato stem. For our early ancestors, it was safer for the amygdala to mistake a plant stem for a poisonous spider than wait for the cortex to assess the situation before reacting. It could be the difference between life and death.

Awareness of these rapid responses initiated by the reactive route can help us understand and cope with the symptoms created by the fight, flight or freeze response, including the most extreme reaction: a panic attack. The amygdala reacts faster than the cortex and has more connections running from the amygdala to the cortex than the other way around. This enables the amygdala to hijack our thinking, overriding other responses, so there is no logical reasoning, just an automatic reaction.

This is vital when saving our lives (we don't want to notice the nice tailored jacket of an attacker when he is running towards us), but it makes it almost impossible for us to reason away this type of anxiety and make sense of why it is happening.

So, while cortex-based strategies are more popular, practising techniques that can counter reactive pathway anxiety and train our brains to stop responding unnecessarily is also essential.

How the Reactive Route Learns What is Dangerous

There are two ways in which the amygdala decides what information is dangerous.

1. Instinct

What sort of information does the amygdala respond to? Research shows we appear predisposed to some dangers that have helped us survive and evolve. We react rapidly to snakes, insects, animals, angry faces, and contamination with little hesitation.[6] However, with training and experience, even these instinctual fears can be overcome. It's common to have animals living with us in our houses as pets and for people to handle snakes and spiders without fear.

2. Emotional Memories

In addition to these predisposed fears, the primary way the amygdala learns about what is dangerous is through emotional memories using the process of association. These could be emotional memories you may or may not remember, as the cortex and the amygdala use separate memory systems.

The amygdala's memory system doesn't contain images or verbal information; you experience it directly as an emotional state. This is why you sometimes may experience anxiety without knowing why. Maybe a particular smell, location, situation, or object may make you feel anxious for no logical reason that comes to mind. This is the emotional memory of the amygdala at work.

Therefore, an object may not be threatening in itself for fear to be associated with it, as the amygdala can link it to an emotional memory. If others ridiculed a person at a party while a particular song was playing in the room, just hearing that song in the future may make that person feel anxious, even if they do not recall why.

It can also work the other way, in that a smell, sight, object, or situation may be associated with positive feelings. A loving grandmother may have worn a particular fragrance when handling you as a baby. Now, you associate that smell with the feeling of love and security, even though you may not recall your grandmother wearing that perfume or even picking you up as a baby. The reactive pathway is responsible for many of our emotional reactions, both positive and negative.

Managing Reactive Route Anxiety

The amygdala learns through experience that something is dangerous or upsetting, so using therapies or interventions that target anxious thinking to overcome anxieties caused by the amygdala route isn't likely to be successful. We're focusing on the wrong route. So, how do we learn to manage amygdala-based anxiety effectively? There are two main ways:

1. Managing Through Awareness

First of all, we must recognise it's amygdala-based anxiety we're experiencing and understand that using the cortex to provide logical explanations for this type of anxiety isn't likely to help; on the contrary, it can often make the anxiety worse.

A person attending a large social gathering or party may feel their heart rate rapidly increasing, their breathing becoming shallower, and their hands shaking as they enter a room full of strangers. This is the reactive route at work. What is the amygdala trying to protect this person from? As mentioned earlier, bumping into a group of strangers in prehistoric times was uncommon and dangerous, and there was a good chance we would be robbed, beaten or even murdered. One of the amygdala's roles is to prevent us from being prey to a predator, and it can often mistake a safe, modern-day environment for a dangerous one. The anxious reaction may also result from an emotional memory of a time when the person had a negative experience in a similar situation in the past.

The person attending the party is unaware the amygdala is automatically reacting to protect them from perceived danger. In a situation like this, the thought route will use the cortex to create reasons for the anxious reaction, such as '*I feel this way because I'm worried people will ignore me if I introduce myself*', '*They all seem more competent than me, I'm likely to make a fool of myself if I talk to someone.*' The more the person focuses on these logical cortex-based explanations for their anxiety, the more anxiety they will create, adding to the original problem. Being aware of the amygdala's ability to take charge is essential.

If we find ourselves in a situation like this, we need to be aware our amygdala is trying to protect us, but what we're experiencing isn't life-threatening. The party may have been important in the previous example, but it was unlikely to mean life or death. So, the person must accept that the physical reactions were due to the amygdala trying to protect them. While these reactions would be helpful if they needed to fight or flee, this isn't a dangerous situation, and coming up with logical explanations for it will only add to the anxiety. This is why, when people experience panic attacks, having someone logically explain why they shouldn't be panicking doesn't help. They're talking to a cortex switched off or overpowered by the amygdala.

Recognise your amygdala is trying to protect you, but it can often be wrong. You don't want your thinking to add fire to the flames. We need to recognise when the amygdala is misreading the situation and sounding the alarm for no reason. I'll explain how we can quieten these thoughts from the cortex and reduce their influence later in the *Three Key Skills: Dealing with Anxious Thoughts and Feelings* part of the book. Also, if your reaction isn't overwhelmingly strong, it's likely to be a challenge response, which can help us perform better in challenging circumstances. We'll discuss this in more detail in *Chapter 7: The Power of Mindset*.

Awareness that the situation is not dangerous and it's just your amygdala kicking in and raising the alarm won't always remedy the situation and stop an overwhelming response. However, awareness is a crucial first step. In some situations, a further successful approach is to use deep breathing techniques or to engage in physical activity; these techniques can engage the parasympathetic nervous system and bring you out of the fight, flight or freeze response, calming the mind. We go through these and other practical exercises in more detail in the *Emergency Exercises: Managing Fight, Flight, or Freeze* part of the book.

2. Managing by Learning Through Experience

To further reduce or eliminate unhelpful amygdala-based anxiety, you have to use the language of the amygdala rather than the cortex, and that means learning through experience. If, for example, you want to change the amygdala's anxiety response to talking to a stranger at a party, you must activate the memory circuits that relate to talking to strangers, and only then can new connections be made and the amygdala taught to respond differently. If you want to change the amygdala's anxiety response to public speaking, you must activate the memory circuits that relate to public speaking.

We mentioned experience-dependent neuroplasticity earlier in the book. This process allows the brain to make new connections, alter the circuitry, and change the amygdala's future responses.

People will, understandably, often try to avoid these challenging and anxiety-inducing situations, but avoiding them stops the amygdala from forming new connections and responding differently. The amygdala tries to preserve learned emotional reactions by avoiding exposure to the triggers. This decreases the likelihood of any neural changes or the elimination of anxiety. By exposing ourselves to situations or objects that make us anxious but challenging that association – by realising nothing terrible happens – we can develop new connections in the amygdala that compete with and eventually overpower those that create fear and anxiety.

If we see anxiety-inducing situations as an opportunity to learn, change, and rewire our neural pathways, we can motivate ourselves to confront them. Although challenging, if we nurture an opportunity mindset and understand that exposing ourselves to the anxiety that arises will produce positive neuroplastic changes, we can grasp the courage to face our fears and become unstuck. We'll address how to take action despite feeling anxiety and fear in *Part 4: Action Mode: A Step-By-Step Social Anxiety Action Plan*.

～

2. THE THOUGHT ROUTE

When we think of anxiety, we usually associate it with cortex-based anxiety, the type of anxiety created by anxious thinking. We're more consciously aware of this type of anxiety and can recognise it in our thoughts and feelings. This is because the cortex is more directly under our control than the amygdala. As a result, we're able to train ourselves to be aware of, interrupt, and change anxious thoughts and images, and therefore reduce our anxiety. However, this isn't always easy, as we develop long-standing patterns of thinking and ingrained habits.

The cortex can influence our anxiety in two main ways. Firstly, as described earlier, it can worsen anxiety in the amygdala by creating unhelpful and inaccurate reasons for our anxious feelings. Secondly, it can independently initiate unnecessary anxiety using thoughts and images.

How the Thought Route Initiates Anxiety

The cortex can initiate unnecessary anxiety using thoughts and images in two main ways.

Firstly, it interprets neutral or harmless sensory information (sights, sounds, smells, touch) provided by the thalamus as threatening and then sends this information to the amygdala to produce anxiety.

For example, you're walking through a restaurant when you notice someone look up at you, smirk, and shake their head. You immediately wonder why they don't like you, what they find so amusing, and why they're dismissing you. You get closer to the person and realise they're in deep conversation on their phone and unaware of you.

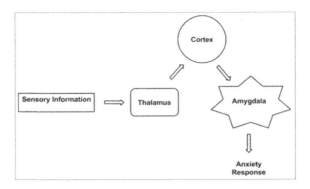

The second way the cortex initiates anxiety using thoughts and images is by independently producing distressing thoughts without receiving sensory information.

You're due to deliver a presentation at work in a few days, and while lying in bed, you imagine that you'll forget some of your main points and panic in front of everyone. Your cortex sends this information to your amygdala, and an anxiety response is triggered, even though no sensory information has been provided about your presentation.

The amygdala responds to imaginary information in the same way it responds to a real situation. Hence, anxiety brought about by thoughts and images created in the cortex is just as strong as the anxiety you will experience from an actual situation or threat.

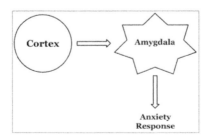

We often worry this way, hoping the rumination will lead to a solution or help guard us against future negative events. We can sometimes come up with novel solutions through worrying, but we rarely do. More often than not, we strengthen the neural pathways in the cortex that create worry. Due to neuroplasticity, whatever you devote a lot of time to thinking about in great detail is more likely to be strengthened, creating a vicious circle.

Managing Thought Route Anxiety

We can learn some key skills to help us effectively manage anxious thinking. Remember, in the thought route, the cortex initiates anxiety in one of two ways: by interpreting neutral sensory information as dangerous and sending this information to the amygdala to produce anxiety or by creating anxious thoughts and feelings on its own, without sensory information, and again, sending this information to the amygdala to produce anxiety.

So, we need to learn to manage unhelpful thoughts and images in a way that will eliminate the anxiety response of the amygdala or reduce its strength. This will enable us to take control of our behaviour and engage fully with our actions rather than entering safety mode and allowing our anxiety to lead the way.

Before we outline these essential skills, let's investigate some common solutions we are told can help reduce negative thoughts. The advice often tells us to:

- Challenge or dispute the thoughts by looking for evidence to demonstrate that they aren't true.
- Replace negative thoughts with positive thoughts.
- Distract ourselves from these thoughts.

You may have tried one or more of these strategies before, and if so, you may have recognised some common problems with these approaches:

- They require a lot of effort and energy and can divert you from your original intention.
- They focus your mind on the negative thoughts.
- They only give you temporary relief before your mind develops new negative thoughts.
- When you leave your comfort zone to enter a challenging situation, they don't work.

If these methods don't work as long-term strategies, what's the alternative? Well, there's a radically different way of responding to negative thoughts that may seem counterintuitive.

The approach comes from Acceptance and Commitment Therapy (often abbreviated to ACT) — an evidenced-based psychological intervention that uses acceptance and mindfulness strategies to overcome anxiety and manage stress.[7] ACT suggests we can reduce the influence of negative thoughts and anxious feelings without trying to get rid of them. This method works even though it makes no effort to reduce, challenge, eliminate, or change negative thoughts. Why? Because it starts from the assumption that negative thoughts are not inherently problematic.

In his book, *The Happiness Trap*, leading ACT practitioner Dr Russ Harris explains that negative thoughts are only considered problematic if we get caught up in them, give them all of our attention, treat them as the absolute truth, allow them to control us, or get in a fight with them. You may remember from earlier that when we get caught up in our thoughts, give them all of our attention, and consider them the absolute truth, we're deemed to be FUSING with them. When two things fuse, they become joined together. When we're caught up in our thoughts this way, we are cut off or disconnected from what is happening right in front of us, making engaging with our environment difficult. Our anxious thoughts become our reality and dominate our behaviour.

The ACT approach teaches three key skills to help us effectively manage cortex-based anxiety: **defusion**, **expansion**, and

engagement. We'll briefly outline these skills next and return to them later in the book to explain how we can apply them.

1. Defusion

To counteract unhelpful thoughts, we can defuse or separate from them. When we defuse thoughts, we become aware that they are nothing more or less than words and pictures and can have little or no effect on us, even if they are true.

As an analogy, imagine you're driving a bus while all the passengers (thoughts) are noisily chattering, being critical, or shouting out directions. You can allow them to shout but choose not to engage with them, keeping your attention focused on the road ahead. If you turn around and argue with the passengers, you may have to stop the bus or become distracted and make a wrong turn. So you keep driving, allowing them to shout, but safe in the knowledge they can't hurt you. You defuse them.

2. Expansion

When our cortex provides unhelpful thoughts, we often experience uncomfortable feelings. As mentioned earlier, we usually do our best to avoid these feelings or sensations, trying to distract ourselves from them or get rid of them. However, we can learn to deal with them effectively by using expansion—the ability to open up and make room for emotions, sensations, and feelings.

So we accept they are there and allow them to pass through without impacting our behaviour. When we experience anxious feelings, we don't battle with them but accommodate them and allow them to come and go in their own time. It doesn't mean we want them, like them, or approve of them, but we stop investing our time and effort in fighting them. The more space we can give the difficult feelings, the smaller their influence and impact on our lives.

3. Engagement

The next step is engaging with experiences, tasks, and situations despite unhelpful thoughts and uncomfortable feelings. Engagement is being present and actively involved in what we are doing – not lost in our thoughts. Being anxious is not a problem, but disengaging from our experience is.

The more we focus on unhelpful thoughts and unpleasant feelings, the more we disconnect from the present moment. This particularly tends to happen with social anxiety. We get hooked on stories about the future, how things might go wrong, and how badly we will handle them. We don't have to be connected to the present moment all the time, but it is beneficial to do so in some situations, particularly when anxiety is diverting us away from our desired behaviour.

In *Three Key Skills: Dealing with Anxious Thoughts and Feelings*, we will discuss the details and practicalities of defusion, expansion, and engagement and also try several different exercises to see what works best for you.

So far, we've discussed how and why anxiety develops, described the routes it takes, and outlined how we can start to manage our anxiety. Before starting the practical journey and beginning the exercises, we're first going to raise awareness of how anxiety can progress in a way that seriously impacts our lives. Shining a light on how anxiety can become a disorder can help to take us out of automatic pilot and stop our anxiety in its tracks before it becomes a significant problem.

SIX

When Social Anxiety Gets Serious

HOW SOCIAL ANXIETY CAN DEVELOP INTO A DISORDER

Everyone experiences social anxiety from time to time. It can often be situation specific — if we're facing an interview, attending a social event alone, or performing a difficult task in front of others — or sometimes, there are periods in our lives when we feel a little more anxious than at other times. However, occasionally, social anxiety can appear more permanent and affect every part of our lives. How do we go from temporary or situation-specific anxiety to developing an anxiety disorder?

ESCAPE AVOIDANCE LEARNING

Most anxiety disorders develop through what psychologists call Escape Avoidance Learning, which follows this general pattern:

1. **Situation.** Let's say something happened at a cinema when I was a child. Maybe I tripped over when waiting in line to buy a ticket, spilling the popcorn I was holding onto the floor, and the other people in the line laughed at me. I suppressed it, as when I was younger, it was embarrassing and painful. Now, much later on in

life, I visit the cinema, and I'm in a line waiting to buy tickets and smell popcorn.

2. **Anxiety**. The smell of popcorn may be enough to bring up some sense of anxiety, as this is how associational memory works. It only takes a small trigger to connect us back to something difficult or unpleasant.

3. **Unpleasant feelings.** I find the anxiety unpleasant, especially if I'm having some physiological response (heart beating rapidly, shallow breathing). I may feel like I'm going to have a panic attack.

4. **Leave situation.** I want to get rid of the unpleasant sensation, so I decide I will get away from the situation by leaving the lobby, or I may even leave the cinema altogether.

5. **5. Anxiety goes**. Once outside in the car park, I start to feel better and notice a reduction in my anxiety.

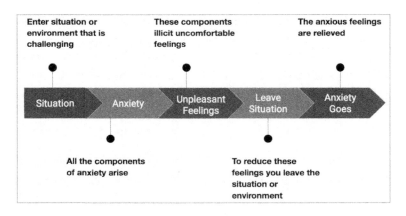

Negative Reinforcement

As I found relief from my anxiety by leaving the situation, I'm more likely to repeat this behaviour in the future. This is called negative reinforcement — the reinforcement that comes from removing an unpleasant experience. So the next time I go to the cinema and smell popcorn, I'll be more likely to do the same thing because it feels good to have the negative experience stop. This can also extend to other situations; I may avoid the post office and shopping on the high street. In extreme cases, this can lead to fully-blown Social Anxiety Disorder.

Even though the behaviour may not develop into something as serious as Social Anxiety Disorder, most of us develop these little patterns around things we're afraid of and start to avoid situations that make us feel anxious. This is then negatively reinforced and causes limiting and problematic behaviour. We don't face our fears; we avoid or distract ourselves from them. So, how is anxiety like this usually treated?

EXPOSURE AND RESPONSE PREVENTION

In the 1980s, a number of universities started exploring interventions for anxiety and phobias created by specific situations.[8] Many of the universities experimented treating people with snake phobias to investigate and illustrate how anxiety caused by Escape Avoidance Learning can be treated. Although the experiments didn't investigate social anxiety specifically, the same principles apply to any type of anxiety. The interventions were generally designed using the following pattern:

1. The participants would arrive at the university and be told by a researcher that a snake is locked in a cage in a room some distance away.
2. In the early days of this research, a relaxation method called 'reciprocal inhibition' was used. This involved the participants being trained to reduce their anxiety using a muscle relaxation technique. However, later on in the research, it was discovered that this step wasn't necessary, and participants were encouraged to stay with the experience and allow the anxiety to be there until it went by itself.

3. With the snake still in a distant room, the researcher talked to the participant, described the snake, answered any questions, and waited until nothing happened, and the anxiety declined.
4. The snake was then moved to a closer room, and the participant was given time to calm down. Step by step, the snake was moved closer until it was brought into the same room and put in front of the participant.
5. Eventually, the participant would handle the snake.

It was discovered if you repeat this exercise several times, the person would eventually lose their snake phobia. The anxiety response became extinguished because the participant experienced nothing terrible happened. This approach has since been found to work for nearly all phobias. This is an example of the amygdala learning from experience. It works by activating the memory circuits that cause the anxiety and then allowing learning to rewire the neural pathways and eliminate or reduce the anxiety response.

Often, when people seek treatment for social anxiety, they aren't initially interested in 'handling the snake'. They don't want the treatment to feel uncomfortable or to face their fears. People want to get rid of their anxious feelings without feeling discomfort, but there is no magic bullet for treating social anxiety. Like the people who handled the snake, this book focuses on teaching us to increase our capacity to bear anxiety and to change our relationship with the experience.

Later in the book, in chapters 14 and 15, we'll examine learning through experience in more detail. The chapters explain how we can use exposure treatment to design a Social Anxiety Action Plan and practically apply it in social situations that cause us anxiety.

When we use specific interventions and mindfulness-based exercises to treat our social anxiety, research indicates they can go further than just improving our experience of anxiety. With consistent practice, we can change the structure and functioning of our brain in ways that benefit us beyond our mental health. In the next part, we'll introduce exercises that will create a solid foundation by calming the mind, increasing energy, and preparing you for the mindfulness skills introduced in the next section. We'll start by looking at the power of mindset.

PART II
Preparing for Change

BUILDING A FOUNDATION FOR BEHAVIOUR CHANGE

SEVEN

The Power of Mindset

When people struggle with anxiety, they often can't see a way out, thinking life will always be this way. It may be because anxiety has been a part of their lives for so long, or they believe it's a fixed personality trait and change is impossible. While genetics can predispose us to anxiety, it's our experiences, lifestyle, and behaviour patterns that determine whether we 'switch on' the genes. So, there is much we can do to help ourselves.

Short-term strategies may help us to 'get by' and overcome certain situations, but sufferers often can't imagine a life free from everyday debilitating anxiety. Whilst we will never eliminate anxiety - neither should we want to - it is possible to change our relationship with it in a fundamental way.

Acceptance of who we are and how we feel is essential. However, before we identify too strongly with our anxiety and label ourselves as lifelong members of the anxiety club, we should consider the possibilities that a change of mindset can bring.

Later, we will examine the importance of having a growth mindset—a set of beliefs that change is possible through learning and action—instead of a fixed mindset, the belief that our traits and abilities are fixed. First, we will focus on the evidence demonstrating the powerful impact our beliefs can have on our body, brain, and behaviour.

Recent research investigating the effect of mindset on health has revealed that our beliefs and attitudes can change how the body responds to physical and mental threats and directly impact our well-being. Studies by Harvard University psychologists Alia Crum and Ellen Langer, highlighted in Kelly McGonigal's excellent book *The Upside of Stress*,[9] have demonstrated that changing the way we think about an experience can change the way our bodies react to it.

The research is remarkable and surprising and will make you think twice about your beliefs. When I first discovered the research, it changed the way I thought about my anxiety. Before focusing on stress and anxiety, we'll briefly examine how mindset affects physical health and hunger.

MINDSET AND PHYSICAL HEALTH

Crum and Langer's research first came to my attention when I was preparing a health psychology module for undergraduate students in 2007. The findings of their first mindset study made me scratch my head in disbelief.

The researchers recruited hotel maids to investigate if a change in mindset could lead to a change in physical health.[10] Before starting the intervention, two-thirds of the maids believed they weren't exercising regularly. Measurements of their physical health reflected this belief: the maids' blood pressure, body weight, and waist-to-hip ratio matched those of sedentary people. This puzzled Crum and Langer because the work the maids were doing was strenuous, burning over 300 calories an hour (in comparison, the average office worker burns only 100 calories an hour).

They divided the hotel maids into two groups: an experimental mindset group and a control group. The mindset group attended a talk and was given an information sheet explaining that the work they were doing each day demanded physical exercise that exceeded the Surgeon General's recommendations for an active lifestyle: pushing carts loaded with linen, lifting heavy mattresses, vacuuming, and walking from room to room. They also put posters around the group's workplace detailing how many calories they burned while doing each activity.

The maids in the control group were only informed about the importance of physical exercise for health; they weren't told that their work qualified as exercise.

At the end of the study, four weeks later, the hotel maids in the mindset group had shown remarkable improvements in their physical health; their blood pressure had dropped, they had lost weight, and they had reduced their body fat. These changes happened with no extra physical exercise being completed inside or outside of their work and no change in diet. The control group showed no changes in physical health over the same four-week period.

The study appeared to indicate that our expectations and beliefs about our behaviour—our mindset—can influence physical outcomes. Put another way, 'the effect you expect is the effect you get.'

MINDSET AND HUNGER

To test these mindset findings further, Crum and colleagues designed a study to test if people's perceptions of how calorific a particular food is can affect their levels of fullness and hunger.[11] They gave participants two different milkshakes; one was described as an indulgent treat high in calories and fat, and the other was described as a healthy diet shake with low calories and low fat. However, the milkshakes were precisely the same; they were just labelled differently. The researchers also measured the changes in the participants' blood levels of ghrelin — a hormone associated with hunger. When blood levels of ghrelin go down, we feel full and sated; when they rise, we feel hungry.

The measurements found that when the participants believed they had drank an indulgent high-calorie shake, their ghrelin levels dropped three times as much as when they thought they were drinking a low-calorie shake. Remember, when ghrelin levels go down, we feel full. The participants also reported feeling fuller and less hungry after the high-calorie shake. So, the findings weren't just based on self-reported perceptions; the different perceptions resulted in hormonal changes. Their expectations altered the levels of their hormones.

In both studies—the hotel maid study and the milkshake study—the participants' body responses changed when their mindset—their perceptions—changed. A change in mindset resulted in the body reacting in an adaptive or more helpful way. Perceiving physical work as exercise helped the body experience the benefits of being active, and viewing a milkshake as a high-calorie indulgence helped the body produce signals of fullness.

MINDSET AND STRESS

However, a later study investigating stress interested me the most. Knowing stress can be beneficial and harmful, Crum and colleagues wondered if changing how people thought about stress would change how the body responded. Can mindset affect how the body experiences stress? To examine this question, they manipulated people's views of stress and then measured how their bodies reacted to a stressful situation.[12]

Again, they divided participants into two groups. One group watched a three-minute video presenting research outlining stress's benefits: improving performance and making us more focused, alert, and competitive. The other group watched a three-minute video presenting research outlining stress's negative and debilitating aspects.

Both videos were based on fundamental research because stress can be helpful and unhelpful. However, the videos were also designed to prime the participants' perceptions into a positive or negative mindset. After watching the video, both groups were subjected to tough mock interviews, with interviewers trained to give negative and critical feedback to the participants throughout.

Samples of two stress hormones were also taken from both groups before and after intervention. The hormones measured were cortisol and dehydroepiandrosterone (DHEA). Cortisol turns sugar and fat into energy and directs the body to use that energy when stressed while also suppressing some biological functions, such as digestion and reproduction. DHEA is a neurosteroid—a hormone that helps the brain grow stronger from stressful experiences. It also counters some of the effects of cortisol, speeds up the repair of wounds, and improves immune function.

We need both hormones when experiencing stress. Each has an important role, so neither can be categorised as good or bad. However, the ratio between the hormones can influence the long-term impact of stress, especially when stress is chronic, long-lasting and consistently occurring over time.

High levels of cortisol over long periods have been linked with weakened immune function and depression, but high levels of DHEA are associated with reductions in anxiety, depression, heart disease, and other diseases we associate with stress. The ratio of DHEA to cortisol is called the growth index of a stress response, and the more DHEA is present, the higher the growth index. High growth indexes have been shown to help people flourish under stress, increase resilience, and support recovery.

To summarise, a greater ratio of DHEA to cortisol in the stress response creates a higher growth index, and a higher growth index is beneficial for the body, reducing the impact of the stress response and protecting the body from many of the diseases associated with stress.[13]

The study's preliminary results indicated that the type of

video a participant watched did not affect cortisol, which rose in both groups during the mock interview. However, there were higher levels of DHEA and, therefore, a higher growth index in the group that watched the video, informing them that stress was beneficial. The results suggested that viewing stress as helpful created a different biological reality, again demonstrating that expectations can alter hormones and help the body become more adaptive.

The next step in the research was to discover whether these changes in mindset were long-lasting or only temporary.

CHANGES IN MINDSET ARE LONG-LASTING

Further studies by Crum and colleagues have shown that changing a person's mindset has a long-lasting impact on their lives and is not just specific to one event. So altering an individual's mindset about stress doesn't just help them cope with the stress of a one-time mock interview but influences their beliefs and physical reactions to stress in other stressful situations over a longer time.

The research has also demonstrated that people who believe stress can be beneficial have fewer health problems and cope better with challenges than those who see stress as harmful. It's not that they are less stressed; the research shows they are, in fact, just as stressed as the people who don't cope as well, but they interpret the stress response differently and can manage it more effectively.

Stress mindsets are powerful because they affect not just how we think but how we act, too. If we believe stress is harmful, we are also more likely to become anxious and distract ourselves from dealing with stressful and problematic situations rather than tackling them and sorting them out. So, instead of dealing with the source of the anxious feelings, we focus on getting rid of them, and we sometimes do this in maladaptive ways, like avoidance or turning to food, alcohol, or other substances.

On the other hand, when we see stress as beneficial or enhancing, we don't try to distract ourselves from feeling anxious or try to avoid it, but accept it's real and plan a strategy for dealing with the situation. People with this mindset often seek help or advice and take steps to tackle the source of the anxiety, viewing it as an opportunity to grow and improve. So mindset changes can be considered catalysts; they put processes into motion that create and maintain positive changes over time.

CHANGING OUR MINDSET

People have difficulty accepting brief interventions can change a mindset because they believe meaningful problems are deep rooted and difficult to change. However, changing a mindset isn't some magical manipulation; it's about educating people and showing them they have a choice about what to believe. The most successful interventions designed to change mindsets have three stages:[14]

- Firstly, people are educated, and learn the new point of view.
- Secondly, they participate in an exercise encouraging them to apply the new mindset.
- Finally, they are given the opportunity to share the idea with others.

In the case of changing an individual's mindset about stress, firstly, they would learn the benefits of feeling stressed. They would then be given a chance to adopt the new mindset in a stressful situation, and finally, they would be encouraged to share and explain their new mindset with others. This is precisely what happened in Crum and Langer's stress study. So, in what way can anxiety and stress be beneficial?

THE BENEFITS OF STRESS

Over the following few chapters, we will consider when and how social anxiety can be problematic and debilitating. We will also discuss the stress response in greater detail throughout the book. Having discussed how vital mindset is—our beliefs about anxiety—let's first talk about how anxiety and stress can be beneficial.

The stress response is also called the emergency arousal system and the fight, flight or freeze response. It's vital to survival, managing challenging situations, and how we relate to others (more of this later). So we should see it as our friend and appreciate it. Its intention is to keep us safe from danger and help us perform at our best when challenged. The stress response can be initiated by anxiety about a potentially threatening situation as well as a reaction to being in an actual threatening situation.

The Challenge Response

Not every response we have to anxiety-inducing situations is an all-or-nothing fight-or-flight response. We have understandable stress responses when important things are at stake, but there is some nuance in our stress response. When there is a real threat to our survival, we will experience the full fight, flight or freeze response, along with strong biological changes. However, when the situation is less threatening, we tend to experience a challenge response. The muscles and brain get more energy, heart rate increases, and adrenaline is released. These changes help us perform better under pressure and in stressful situations, giving us a detailed focus of attention, more energy, heightened senses, and greater motivation.

Connection and Courage

An often overlooked hormone released in the stress response is oxytocin. When oxytocin is released into the bloodstream, it motivates us to seek out social connections while raising our levels of empathy, trust, and intuition. This is why we often seek out others to talk to or be with when we feel challenged or stressed. Recent research has shown that contrary to most people's expectations when people are caught up in traumatic events, such as a terror attack, they are more likely to help each other rather than act only in their best interests.[15] However, more than just seeking out social connection, oxytocin also dampens the fear response in the brain, increasing courage and suppressing the urge to fight or flee.

Learning and Recovery

Experiencing a stress response also prepares us for similar future stressful situations, and expecting to learn from stressful situations can give us a type of stress inoculation. Just like vaccinations protect or inoculate us from future illness by stimulating our immune systems to develop immunity. The brain does this by using the previously mentioned DHEA and nerve growth factor, which is released in the stress response to increase the brain's ability to learn and change. These hormones also speed up physical and mental recovery, helping us to bounce back from challenging situations.

This is often why, for several hours after a stressful event, we repeatedly review it in our minds — time and time — considering how we responded, what actions we did, and what thought processes we used. We talk to others about it and experience intense emotions of relief, shock, joy, and anger. All of this makes the experience more memorable, allowing it to change the brain to be better equipped to respond to similar situations in the future.

This is why many professionals are encouraged to practice skills, techniques, and actions in stressful situations. Footballers practice penalty kicks in front of crowds, and emergency service responders practise procedures in challenging environments. Going through a stressful situation can make us better at responding to similar challenging situations. If we see anxiety-inducing situations as opportunities to improve, grow, and become better at challenges, we are less likely to avoid or distract ourselves from them.

A GROWTH MINDSET

We've made the case that anxiety and stress can be beneficial in certain circumstances, not that the way we experience it is always helpful, and we should accept it as it is and do nothing about it. As we will find out, it also can be debilitating and overwhelming, especially when our anxiety triggers a full fight, flight or freeze response when it's not needed.

If you suffer from anxiety in this way or are often troubled by anxious thoughts that make life difficult, the idea of anxiety being beneficial may sound ridiculous, and the suffering you've endured over time may have left you feeling hopeless.

However, it isn't suffering that leads to hopelessness; it's suffering you think you can't control. The exercises in this book will provide you with hope. Not a magical positive thinking type of hope, but a real and practical hope. So it's important you approach the following chapters with an understanding that:

- Anxiety isn't all bad. Changing the way we think about anxiety is the first step to overcoming it.
- Change is possible. Our abilities, skills, emotions, and behaviour are not fixed. Through learning, effort, and application, we can change, grow and transform our relationship with anxiety and be our best selves.

EIGHT

Being Confident in Who You Are

This chapter starts the practical journey this book will take you on. It's about considering and understanding who you are, discovering your values, and gaining confidence by behaving in a way that is consistent with who you are rather than by pleasing others. Although you may be keen to tackle anxious thoughts and feelings immediately, it's essential you first build a foundation that will hold you steady when faced with the challenge of changing your relationship with your social anxiety.

Uncovering our values has two significant benefits. Firstly, research has shown that people who live a life aligned to their values have better physical and mental health, including lower levels of anxiety.[16] Secondly, when people are asked to consider their most deeply held values, they become less defensive and more open to change. Studies show that people are more successful in quitting smoking, exercising, and changing their diet if asked to consider their values first.[17] It's much easier to make difficult choices and follow through with successful behaviour if these actions align with your values. This is beneficial as we're about to embark on changing your relationship with social anxiety.

Who Are You?

We can know ourselves better by asking ourselves what matters and determining what we value. By spending a little time reflecting on, and perhaps writing about, who we think we are, we can reduce our hormonal anxiety and be more present and effective in challenging environments. Studies have shown that when people write about their authentic selves before entering a potentially anxious situation, they have significantly lower cortisol levels — a hormone we release when we feel under stress — than people who don't.[18]

So, affirming our values has the benefit of making us more open to change while also reducing our anxiety in challenging situations. This is not about psyching ourselves up and exclaiming 'I'm the best!' or 'I'm a winner!' as we traditionally think about expressing positive affirmations. It's more about appreciating that our best selves emerge when we have full access to our values, traits, and strengths and know we can express them through our actions. In other words, it's understanding who we truly are and having the confidence to be authentic. These affirmations help us believe in and clarify our own stories. This allows us to trust that who we are will come naturally through what we say and do. We will never overcome our social anxiety by pretending to be someone else.

While on one of my daily dog walks, I listened to a podcast by the rapper Scroobious Pip (real name David Meads), in which he interviewed the author Jon Ronson.[19] They were both talking about their experiences with anxiety (Ronson has written in great detail about his paralysing levels of social anxiety), and Scroobious Pip remarked he had lost confidence when a relationship ended out of the blue. He described how, during this period of anxiety, he spent a week writing and recording a song (that wasn't released commercially). Pip explained how this process reminded him of who he is and his values and strengths. He said the project helped him to recover his confidence. In the following exercise, we will remind ourselves who we are, what we value, and what is important to us.

It's essential we don't just reflect on our values without taking practical steps to try to understand them fully. We can do this by writing about them. Writing is a powerful exercise because it serves to clarify our thoughts and feelings in a way reflection alone cannot. In the act of writing, ideas emerge and are shaped, and this gives us a clearer understanding of who we are.

Preparing to Change Exercise 1: Who Are You?

A printable template of this exercise can also be found online using the link below. Just type the exact link into your web browser to access the template: http://bit.ly/2rY7BC

Step 1: Consider your values. The table below lists some of the most common core values. Choose one or two values you feel are most central to your identity, closest to the core of who you are.

Dependable	Loyal	Efficient
Inspiring	Reliable	Committed
Adventurous	Passionate	Serving
Creative	Motivated	Respectful
Consistent	Humorous	Positive
Hardworking	Honest	Witty
Respected	Educated	Loving
Fit	Courageous	Fun-loving
Innovative	Open-minded	Kind
Athletic	Optimistic	Nurturing

The list is to help you reflect. You don't have to choose from the list if you know of values you possess that aren't listed.

Core value 1: _____ Core value 2: _____

Step 2: Then, write a short note on why these values are important to you and a particular time when they proved to be important. A person who deeply values being humorous might write:

"Being funny around others is important to me. I believe we all would be better off if we sometimes took life a bit less seriously. I enjoy making people laugh, it makes me feel good, and it comes easily to me. I remember being out with my colleagues from work, and we had all been stressed, but I found humour in how difficult things were at the time, and we all ended up laughing. It broke the ice, and we had a great night."

(Core value 1)   is important to me because:

(Core value 1)   proved to be important when:

(Core value 2)   is important to me because:

```
┌─────────────────────────────────────────────┐
│                                             │
│                                             │
│                                             │
│                                             │
└─────────────────────────────────────────────┘
```

(Core value 2)   proved to be important when:

```
┌─────────────────────────────────────────────┐
│                                             │
│                                             │
│                                             │
│                                             │
└─────────────────────────────────────────────┘
```

Notice you only need to affirm your personal core values — not values or abilities relevant to any specific task you need to do or any challenge you are facing. So, for example, if you have an up-and-coming job interview, don't try to convince yourself you'll be successful by choosing values you think are related to the interview or job. The key to this exercise working is knowing who you are and being comfortable and assured of that.

I'd suggest repeating this exercise occasionally, especially when facing an anxious situation or challenge. You could also try a more creative way of reflecting on your core values and strengths by undertaking a project or task that expresses who you are, much like Scroobious Pip did in the example I described above.

What If I Don't Like My Values or Want to Change Them?

Being unsure of our values or feeling we don't like them is a good sign that our true values are the ones we would like to have — the values we aspire to. Just because we currently don't behave in a way that is consistent with those values doesn't mean we don't hold them or can't develop them. They are hidden and need uncovering. If this is the case for you, when you try the exercise above, choose the values you would like to have — the ones that make you the type of person you would like to be.

If you're still struggling to discover your true values, it may be helpful to heed the advice of Warren Buffett, one of the world's most generous philanthropists and a very successful business-man. When addressing Seattle college students in 1998, Buffett suggested that students should look to role models to nurture successful values and habits.

He told them that if they wanted to live purposeful and successful lives, they should think of the person they admired the most, write what they admired about them, and then aim to emulate their values and qualities. He also suggested the students should bring to mind a person they can stand the least, write the qualities and values that turn them off that person, and avoid practising them at all costs.

Buffet's message tells us that with awareness, intention, and practice, we can develop the values, qualities, and habits of those we admire and avoid the ones of those we dislike.

LOOKING OUTWARDS: FOCUSING AWAY FROM YOU AND YOUR ANXIETY

When we're looking to overcome our social anxiety, we often focus intensely on ourselves as we try to find a solution. This is understandable, as anxiety is an individual state. When feeling anxious, it seems reasonable to think we should focus our atten-tion inwards to 'work' on ourselves and assess how effective the strategies and exercises are in helping us.

However, while some self-evaluation is necessary — we need to know what's working after all — intense self-focus has also been shown to harm wellbeing. A wealth of evidence has demon-strated anxiety already turns people inward. It makes us more introspective and, therefore, less socially engaged and lonelier, and this self-focus can also undermine happiness and cause depression.[20] It's like a vicious circle; we feel anxious, so we withdraw and become introspective, which makes us more anxious.

Alongside this, to find out if we're making progress, we often compare our past levels of anxiety to our current levels of anxiety. This creates a problem: the moment we make that comparison, we shift from experiencing life to evaluating life.

Consider the research on flow — a state of complete absorption in an activity. Researchers have found when people are in a flow state, they don't report on any particular emotion — being happy, sad, anxious, fearful — as they're too busy concentrating on the activity. But afterwards, looking back, they describe flow as a positive emotion.

If consumed with evaluating the strategies we're using to help overcome our social anxiety, we can never fully engage in activities, projects, relationships and life in general. Instead, we can become anxious and depressed, entering a vicious circle. This is documented by psychologists Katariina Salmela-Aro and Jari-Erik Nurmi: anxiety and depression lead people to evaluate their daily projects and social engagements as less enjoyable, and ruminating about why they're not fun makes anxiety and depression worse.[21]

So, what can we learn from this research? Firstly, we should engage with exercises and projects without constantly evaluating how anxious we are and focus instead on the exercises or projects themselves—the skills we learn later in the book will help us with this. Some reflection on whether the exercises are effective and which ones work best can be valuable, but we should avoid constantly evaluating our anxiety and happiness.

Secondly, we should be wary of becoming too self-focused or self-absorbed with ourselves and our anxiety and attempt to look outwards towards other people. Some interesting research from the University of British Columbia discovered that encouraging people who suffer from social anxiety to engage with others - through acts of kindness - helped reduce their anxiety.[22] The researchers recruited participants who reported experiencing high levels of social anxiety and randomly assigned them to three groups for a four-week intervention. One group performed acts of kindness, the second group was exposed to social interactions, and the final group was given no instructions except to record what happened each day. The results found that those individuals asked to perform acts of kindness showed the most significant overall decrease in their anxiety about social interactions. They were less scared of and more drawn to socialising with others.

Why is this? The theory behind the results is that anxious people don't socially interact because they try to protect themselves from being evaluated negatively by other people. This means any chance to demonstrate that their perceptions may be wrong is cut off. The acts of kindness helped counter this fear of negative evaluation, as the anxious people found people responded more positively to them than they expected.

We often assume that other people are unfriendly or closed off to interacting with us, and those people think the same of us. Sometimes, it's just a case of making the first move. Some people will rebuff us; we must expect that and dust ourselves off afterwards and try not to judge them. We don't know their circumstances; they may be busy, having a bad day, not feel like talking, or have received bad news. Silently wish them well. However, we will often be surprised how people embrace an interaction when someone else makes the first move. Mindfully engaging with others will increase the chances they'll respond in kind.

When writing this section of the book in the cafe of my local library, I tested this theory. Sitting on the table opposite me was a stern-looking older man in his 70s, intently staring at his cup as he sipped his coffee. I wanted to buy another drink, so, making the social interaction as easy as possible for myself, I asked him if he would mind keeping an eye on my bag when I went to the counter to order another coffee. When I arrived back, I thanked him, and he noticed my Welsh accent. This started a conversation about how we had both ended up in the northern English city of Newcastle (he was from Scotland). He explained that he was here researching his family history.

After this, we often saw each other in the library and sat down for coffee, becoming unlikely friends. Not all of our attempted social interactions will end in longer friendships. It's not always what we want, but it illustrates that people are often, at the very least, happy to talk despite our initial assumptions.

Switch the Spotlight Onto Others

Finally, when out in public and feeling self-conscious about how we look, act, or sound, it is worth remembering that we tend to overestimate how much others notice our actions and appearance. Social psychologists call this the 'spotlight effect.'[23] Most people are so focused on themselves and how they look, act, or speak that they don't notice what we worry about.

We're so terrified of that one-in-100 chance of embarrassment or rejection that we avoid the 99 more likely to be fulfilling interactions. If we focus on saying the right thing, we hardly pay attention to the other person. We're often more concerned about how we think they perceive us than getting to know them. Most people aren't excessively judgmental. They're quick to forgive. And more often than not, they want to connect.

When I started my first university job, I remember arriving in London to meet with other academics at a social event to discuss research. I felt extremely anxious and even considered not showing up, blaming it on a late train. While pondering what to do on my walk to the venue, I noticed graffiti on a wall that said, *'Nobody cares if you don't go to the party.'* On seeing this, I laughed and remembered the research about the spotlight effect; no one would be focused on me as they would all be busy focusing on themselves. This is a phrase I often use when I'm nervous about a social event: *"Calm down, Matt, nobody cares if you don't go to the party."*

A small but valuable advice for people who feel awkward at social gatherings: If you can't think of anything interesting to say about yourself, ask the other person a question instead. How do you know the host? Where are you from? What does that cake taste like?

It sounds like obvious advice, and it is, but often, people don't follow it. Research in social science has found many times over that people are generally pretty bad at guessing how to make a good first impression. The most common mistakes can be grouped under a general 'me, me, me' category. Most people spend most of their conversations sharing their views rather than focusing on the other person. Someone is rarely as interested in you as you are, so if you're worried about people liking you, you can flip your focus from yourself to the person in front of you.

Be Curious About Others

Ask people questions. Be interested in them. Switch the spotlight from you to them. Use open-ended questions often (questions that can't be answered with a yes or no), but not exclusively. You must listen carefully to the responses. Give the other person your full attention. Before this becomes more natural, write down a few possible open-ended questions before social events. You won't likely need to use them, but research shows that knowing you have some prepared questions to fall back on will help you feel at ease and more likely to be present in conversations.

So, while practising all the exercises throughout the book, don't constantly withdraw into your own world; instead, look at how you can help and interact with others.

NINE

Avoiding Exhaustion and Increasing Energy

W hen things get busy, and we're not leading a balanced life, we often let go of the things or activities that nourish us and instead focus on what seems more important or pressing. However, without the things that nourish us, stress increases, and we give up more and more of the activities that replenish us. When this happens, we're only left with work, chores, difficult challenges, or other stressors that deplete our resources, and we can become exhausted or burnt out. Our lives become narrow, and we get stuck in what stress researchers call an *exhaustion funnel*.[24] It's easy to get sucked into this process because we often have pressing demands, and when we do, the more pleasurable things in life seem optional and are easier to give up.

However, despite thinking we have no choice, have too much to do, or don't have the energy to do other things, it is vital we balance our lives during these times, or at the very least spend time on activities that nourish us. Although it may feel counterintuitive, we must make time for replenishment and nourishment to do the other things well and maintain our energy. This will give us the extra time, energy, and perspective required for the challenging parts of our lives.

An experiment at the Bethlehem Steel Company in the 1940s

measured the efficiency of its workers loading pig iron onto trains. On the first day, the men were told to load as much pig iron as they could without stopping. On average, the workers loaded 12.5 tons until exhausted and could do no more. The following day, they were told to load the pig iron for 26 minutes and then rest for 34 minutes, meaning they rested more than they worked. Using this method, each worker managed to load an average of 47 tons, almost four times as much as working flat out.[25]

If you're still unconvinced that balancing your life, resting, and doing things that nourish you is a good idea during busy periods, I'd like to point you in the direction of some research demonstrating why a balanced life is more enjoyable and productive.

Firstly, scientific evidence has emphasised that rest aids decision-making. Research by Dutch psychologist Ap Dijksterhuis (I can't pronounce it either) suggests actively trying to work through decisions, particularly when tired, will lead to a worse outcome than going through all the relevant information and then taking a break or moving on to something else.[26] During rest periods, the subconscious mind can sift through lots of information, and this helps us to make clearer, more helpful decisions. Some of my best ideas and most helpful decisions have come to me when I have been out walking my dog in the countryside after periods of intense work.

Secondly, research has demonstrated that rest replenishes our resources and helps us work more effectively. Attention Restoration Theory (ART)—an area of academic research investigating our ability to maintain attention over time—suggests concentration is limited, and we can exhaust our supply of focused attention. When this happens, we're unable to work effectively or concentrate properly.

Scientists involved in ART research suggest taking regular breaks or switching activities when our attention is tiring. It is particularly recommended that you take a break in nature. This is because there are usually fewer obstacles around open spaces and, therefore, fewer decisions to be made, enabling us to switch off more completely.[27]   However, if taking a break in nature is not possible, we can still be more effective at stressful tasks just by ensuring we take the time to rest or switch to an activity we enjoy, especially something that gives us a break from concentrating or focusing intensely.[28]

Finally, when tired or depleted, our work can often be very low quality. Recent research has indicated that we have a limited capacity to do challenging and demanding work, especially tasks that require our attentional resources.[29] Studies have shown that more often than not, the activities or work we do when we are feeling tired or depleted will be substandard, or at least not our best work.

Additionally, trying to work when depleted often results in errors that must be corrected later or redone. So, staying up late to finish a report for work when feeling tired and depleted will often result in low-quality work that has to be corrected or redone the following day. When extremely busy, while we think we must keep going, we can save time in the long term by taking a break or doing an activity we find nourishing.

This is not just about resting or taking time to relax, although that is vital; it is also about 'play' — taking the time to have fun. The greatest source of nourishment often involves doing things that we enjoy. Think about what you liked to do for fun as a child or teenager when there was no pressure to please anyone else. What did you do with your spare time? Now that you're an adult, what could you do that is similar to that?

THE HIDDEN POWER OF MIRROR NEURONS: THE COMPANY THAT YOU KEEP

When considering activities and situations that nourish or deplete us, we should also reflect on the impact our social relationships can have on us. In the late 1980s, reaching for his lunch, an Italian academic made a remarkable and unexpected discovery about how the behaviours and emotions of others can directly impact us.

Giacomo Rizzolatti and his colleagues implanted electrodes into the brains of macaque monkeys to study their brain activity while performing various motor actions, including clutching food. One day, as a researcher reached for his lunch while glancing at the feedback on his computer screen, he noticed neurons firing in the premotor cortex of one monkey—the area that showed activity when the animals made a similar hand movement. How could this happen when the monkey sat still, not reaching out to grab food but just observing him?

This accidental revelation led to the discovery of mirror neurons — a distinct class of brain cells that fire when an individual performs an action and observes someone else making the same movement. Further research into the workings of mirror neurons demonstrated that this effect goes beyond motor movement. We now know that when we see someone else experiencing an emotion, whether positive or negative, our brain 'tries out' that emotion to imagine what the other person is going through.[30] It does this by trying to fire the same neural pathways in our brains so we can attempt to relate to the emotion we're observing.

This is how we experience empathy and can get caught up in both the positive and negative emotions of others, from angry mob mentality to the solidarity of grief during and after tragedies. It also means we are directly impacted by the attitudes and beliefs of those we spend most time with. If we're continually influenced by critical, cynical, fearful, and pessimistic attitudes, we're constantly firing those synapses in our brain, rewiring it towards anxiety, fear and pessimism rather than peace, confidence and optimism.

So when evaluating our lives and considering how best to balance the activities that nourish and deplete us, we should also consider the company we keep and whether we can take steps to change this, and if not, consider what we can do to improve things. Not that we shouldn't be there for friends who are having a hard time, those who need an empathetic ear or help to work through a difficult situation. I'm also not suggesting we can never be critical or talk about our anxiety, fears or worries, as positive change usually requires critical thought. Only that we should consider who we consistently spend time with and are influenced by.

Preparing to Change Exercise 2: Balancing Life

A printable template of this exercise can also be found online using the link below. Just type the exact link into your web browser to access the template: http://bit.ly/2qHFo1y

Step 1: List your daily activities: Write a list, like the one below, of between 1 and 15 typical activities you do most weeks. Then state which ones nourish you by putting an 'N' in brackets beside the activity, and similarly which ones deplete you by putting a 'D' in brackets.

By nourishing, we mean an activity that lifts your mood, gives you energy or makes you feel calm and centred. Remember, this is not just about rest but also about play. By depleted, we mean an activity that drains you, takes away your energy and makes you tense. There are no right or wrong answers. What may nourish you may deplete someone else and vice versa

Typical Activities
    1. E.g. Constantly checking my email (D)
    2. E.g. Going for a walk (N)
    3. E.g. Checking the news often (D)
    4.
    5.
    6.

Step 2: Redress the balance: There may be some depleting activities you can immediately stop, eliminate, or do less of, and also some nourishing activities you can do more of. Go carefully through the list and make a note of those activities, both depleting and nourishing, that you can change. Don't provide details about how you will do it at this stage; just put a mark next to the activity. You can also consider and note any new activities you don't currently do but know from experience are nourishing for you.

What about unavoidable activities?

There will be some depleting activities you cannot change, especially not immediately (e.g. work, dealing with difficult housemates). If there are depleting activities on your list that are unavoidable, there are a few different approaches you can use:

- First, while you may be unable to avoid some depleting activities altogether, you can try to nudge them down and the nourishing activities up. Some small, subtle changes can make the balance a little better. Think about ways you could do this.
- Secondly, you can try approaching the depleting activities differently. Instead of wishing them away, try being fully present with them, even if you find them boring or unpleasant. You don't have to do this for all unavoidable depleting activities, but try doing it with some and see how you feel.

Step 3: Commit to the changes: Now it's time for you to think about how to alter and commit to the changes that will improve your life balance. Write five ways in which you can practically change things. Don't worry if you can't think of five straightaway; write the others when they come to you later.

It's important to focus on small, doable changes, not life-changing activities. So don't include '*Move to Hollywood*', '*Run a marathon*', or '*Marry Brad Pitt*', but focus on small changes, like the examples below. These small changes are a crucial part of the practice.

I will alter the balance of nourishing and depleting activities by...

1. E.g. Checking my emails only twice a day at 10am and 4pm
2. E.g. Going for a 15-minute walk during my lunch hour and a 30-minute walk on the weekend
3. E.g. Checking the news once or twice a day only.
4. …
5. …
6. …

At first, you may not be aware of which activities nourish or deplete you, so it may be a case of trial and error. Be mindful of this and be open to having some of your preconceived ideas challenged.

We often think some activities are enjoyable, but when we really consider how we feel after them, we realise they deplete us and vice versa. For example, I used to build periods of internet surfing into my day because I thought I found it enjoyable and relaxing. However, when I monitored activities and became aware of how I felt during and after, I realised it often left me feeling tired, unsettled, frustrated, and mildly anxious. Conversely, I used to consider mowing my lawn a depleting activity, but after some reflection, I realised it often left me with a feeling of satisfaction and calmed my mind.

Review your activity lists occasionally, particularly if you feel life is becoming busy, stressful, and unbalanced. Then, consider whether you need to make any further changes.

POWERFUL ESSENTIALS

There are several other things we can do to calm our minds and protect ourselves from constantly teetering near the edge of anxiety and stress. I wanted to keep this book short, simple and manageable, with the intention of not overwhelming people with a whole host of changes that need to be implemented over a short period. This is a recipe for failure. However, it would be remiss of me not to mention a few of the most freely available, cost-effective, and essential contributors to overall well-being and positive mental health: sleep, physical exercise, media diet, and social interaction.

These powerful essentials are often discounted or ignored as people seek a shortcut to good mental health or a magic bullet for social confidence. Putting together a strategy for overcoming anxiety with the best methods and research available but not paying attention to these foundations is like building a solid house on quicksand.

SLEEP

Getting enough sleep is crucial to both our physical and mental health. We can implement every other psychological and physical health strategy to perfection, but if we're not getting enough sleep, we will never be at our best. Research indicates that sufficient sleep significantly affects a whole host of physical and mental aspects of our health. This includes emotion regulation, cognitive thinking, decision-making, attention and memory. It also plays a significant role in protecting the immune system.[31]

Until recently, we knew very little about what happens in the brain when we sleep. Although we still have much to learn, we are starting to understand more about what happens when we go to bed at night.

The Sleep Cycle

We now know we cycle through different periods of sleep several times a night, and in the final stage of each of these cycles, we enter Rapid Eye Movement sleep (REM), the period when dreaming occurs. It's thought REM sleep is essential for our well-being, as it's involved in replenishing our neurotransmitters, cleaning out toxins, and consolidating our memories. Research has also indicated those who have more REM sleep tend to have lower amygdala reactivity and, as a result, less anxiety.[32] A good night's sleep plays a crucial role in calming the amygdala and decreasing anxiety. Lack of sleep increases reactivity in the amygdala, raising our general levels of anxiety and making us more sensitive to other emotional states, such as anger and irritability.

So, how much sleep is sufficient? Eight hours of sleep is usually the magic number suggested to ensure the brain performs at its best. However, recent research suggests it varies from individual to individual, and the optimal time is between seven and nine hours. These recommendations miss out on a critical understanding of the sleep cycle.

The entire sleep cycle lasts around ninety minutes and goes through five stages, with the REM part of the sleep cycle being the last stage:

- **Stage 1**: Light sleep in which we drift in and out of sleep and can be awakened easily.
- **Stage 2**: You are still in light sleep. Your heart rate slows, and your body temperature drops. Your body is getting ready for deep sleep.
- **Stages 3 & 4**: These are the deep sleep stages. Waking in these stages is difficult, as there is no eye movement or muscle activity.

- **REM Stage**: Breathing becomes more rapid, irregular, and shallow. Our eyes jerk rapidly in various directions, and limb muscles become temporarily paralysed. Heart rate also increases, and blood pressure rises. We dream in this stage, and waking during REM sleep often brings bizarre and illogical thoughts as dreams are recalled.

After completing an entire cycle, we return to the first stage and repeat this pattern throughout the night. The first few sleep cycles of the night contain relatively short periods of REM sleep but extended periods of deep sleep. However, as the night progresses, the periods of REM sleep increase in length while deep sleep decreases. By morning, we spend nearly all our sleep time in stages 1, 2, and REM.

If we wake up during one of the ninety-minute cycles, we start again at the first stage when we go back to sleep, regardless of what stage we wake up in. Then, we cycle through the stages until we get to the REM stage again. So, two hours of sleep, followed by a period of being awake, and then another five hours of sleep isn't necessarily the same as seven hours of continuous sleep. You don't carry on where you left off in the cycle; you have to start again at the beginning. Keep this in mind when you're assessing your quality of sleep.

Getting to Sleep When Anxious

Getting a good night's sleep is often a struggle for people with anxiety because the amygdala is regularly in an aroused state, and the sympathetic nervous system is chronically activated. This makes going through the sleep cycles more difficult and is often compounded by worrying thoughts that make it more challenging to drop off. So the key to sleeping well is (1) to ensure you're in as calm a state as possible before going to bed and (2) to find a strategy that enables you to fall asleep without too much trouble.

You may not always have the time to create a calm environment, but it's important to take some time if sleeping is a problem. Once you're able to sleep consistently well, you will be able to be more flexible with your routine.

1. Creating a Calm State

Activities that will help you to enter a calmer state before going to bed include:

View sunlight in the morning: Spend some time outside in the sunlight within the first hours of waking. If it is sunny outside, five to ten minutes is enough. If it is cloudy, aim for 15 minutes if possible. Viewing sunlight in the morning increases early-day cortisol release and prepares the body for sleep later that night. A morning spike in cortisol will also positively influence your immune system, metabolism and ability to focus during the day.

A consistent and relaxing routine before bedtime: Stick to a consistent bedtime on most nights until you start to sleep well. By repeating a regular pattern, you will condition your body and mind to realise it's time to go to sleep. Begin your routine about 30 to 60 minutes before bedtime and build activities into this time that will reduce stimulation and help you relax; such as reading, taking a bath, or listening to music.

Eliminate as much light as possible: Avoid television, computers, tablets and smartphones. Numerous studies suggest blue light in the evening disrupts the brain's natural sleep-wake cycles.[33] If you go online, use an app or software that eliminates blue light on electronic devices. Many can be found by searching for 'blue light' in iPhone and Android app stores.

Create an environment conducive to sleep: Make your bedroom as dark as possible and remove all distractions to sleep out of the bedroom (electronic devices, televisions, work items, etc.).

Avoid caffeine, alcohol, and spicy foods from early evening onwards: These will stimulate your brain and body. Regarding caffeine, research suggests it is beneficial to delay taking your first caffeinated drink until 90 minutes to two hours after waking. This can help reinforce your natural sleep-wake cycle, and you'll be less likely to feel an energy dip around lunch. This can also help you avoid drinking caffeine too close to bedtime.

Exercise earlier in the day: Physical activity will help tire your body and prepare it for sleep. However, exercise no later than early evening to avoid overstimulating your body before bedtime. This doesn't have to involve going to the gym or running for miles. A short, brisk walk can have an excellent impact.

Avoid napping during the day: This is especially important if you're not sleeping well.

Before bed, do some relaxed breathing or a short meditation: Try the *'Panic Attack Exercise 1: Deep Abdominal Breathing'* or the *'Calming the Mind Exercise 1: Mindfulness Meditation'*.

If none of these strategies appeals to you, do anything you want to do before bedtime but ensure that in the last two hours before you attempt to go to sleep, you avoid work, food, exercise, blue light, and pornography (this is not a moral judgement but a strategy to reduce stimulus before bedtime).

2. Strategies to Fall Asleep

While changing your bedtime routine to maximise the chances of going to bed in a calmer state of mind will help with getting to sleep, people who struggle with anxiety often find as soon as they get into bed and can no longer distract themselves, they start worrying or ruminating. This worrying stimulates the cortex, activates the amygdala, and makes dropping off to sleep difficult. So what can we do to help us drop off to sleep quickly?

Some of the traditional methods used for getting to sleep, such as counting sheep, are often ineffective. Knowing we are consciously trying to get to sleep usually makes it difficult, and boredom-inducing strategies tend to make our anxious thoughts even more attractive and often keep us awake longer. However, there are some exercises known to be effective:

Scanning through your day in detail: This exercise involves mentally going through your day in detail, starting from when you woke up. So when you get into bed, close your eyes and recall the very first moment of the day you can remember, and then scan through the day as if you're fast-forwarding a video. Don't do this too quickly. Just do your best to remember all the different parts of the day. It has a certain rhythm to it. So it might be something like this: *I woke up – walked to the bathroom – went to the toilet – brushed my teeth – had a shower – woke my child – went into the kitchen – made breakfast – brushed my teeth – walked to the car – drove to work, and so on.*

Just work your way through the day, remembering everything you did. It should take a few minutes. You may get to parts of the day you'd like to pause and spend a little time thinking about, but don't pause; keep going and leave that behind. Let go of the conversation or situation you'd like to focus on and continue to work your way up to the present time when you're in bed. Notice when your mind wanders off from scanning the day, and when you realise it's wandered, gently bring it back to the scanning, starting from where you left off.

When you've finished scanning through your day, start noticing your breath. Don't change it, but just be aware of it. Count your breaths until you get to ten. If you lose count or your mind wanders, don't worry; bring your attention back to your breath and start again from one.

Cognitive shuffling: This involves mentally picturing a random object for a few seconds before moving on to another: a carton of milk, a car, a castle, a paperclip, and so on. It's vital to ensure the sequence is truly meaningless; otherwise, you'll drift back into rumination.

This method was developed by Canadian cognitive scientist Luc Beaudoin.[34] The exercise is based on the theory that the brain tests whether it's safe to fall asleep by checking what our cortex is doing. If the cortex is engaged in rational thinking, it determines that it may be considering dangers, and it would be best for us to stay awake. However, if the thoughts are random nonsense, the brain finds we are relaxed and tired, and sleep should be induced.

Cognitive shuffling also reduces rumination because it's difficult to focus your attention on more than one thing at a time. Ruminating about a problem at work is hard if you're busy generating images of balloons, cheese, and train carriages. Beaudoin has an app that provides random words and speaks them into your ear. However, I'd suggest avoiding using an app or headphones in bed, as sleep aids like this. While useful for a time, they can act as a crutch and make sleeping without them challenging in the future. Instead, creating these random words yourself would be more effective. Do this by going through the alphabet and naming as many items as you can think of for each letter before going on to the next.

If you're still awake at this stage, count backwards from 100 right the way down to zero, not with the intention of falling asleep but with the intention of getting to zero. If you're still awake after reaching zero, start again at 100, count down again, and keep repeating this.

Sleep meditation: If you still cannot sleep, there is an extended audio guide version of the scanning through your day exercise, with a few extra stages, including a meditation tailored for sleep. You can access and download the exercise here:

https://soundcloud.com/dr-matt-lewis

PHYSICAL ACTIVITY

We all now know physical activity is good for our health. There's growing evidence physical activity can lower the risk of many ailments and disorders, ranging from type 2 diabetes to heart disease to cancer.[35] However, maybe less well known is the gathering evidence illustrating the positive impact of physical exercise on mental wellbeing,[36] and more specifically, anxiety.[37]

Physical Activity Reduces Anxiety Symptoms

Research has shown physical exercise can measurably reduce anxiety in around twenty minutes, which is less time than it takes most medications to work.[38] Physical activity is not only effective at reducing the physiological symptoms of anxiety. It has also been demonstrated to calm the amygdala, reducing its reactivity, meaning anxious feelings and symptoms are less likely to start or are much reduced.[39 & 40]

This shouldn't surprise us, as when anxiety triggers the fight, flight or freeze response, it prepares our body to move quickly and powerfully. Physical activity uses the emergency response in the way it was intended – by moving and being active. Being physically active lowers the levels of adrenaline pumping through the body and uses glucose released into the bloodstream. So exercise calms the amygdala and reduces anxious thoughts and physical symptoms. Significantly, it also positively impacts mental health by producing feelings of well-being and exhilaration, prompted by the release of neurotransmitters called endorphins, which also reduce pain.

However, exercise is not just an antidote to acute anxiety symptoms. It has also been shown to have a long-term effect on anxiety, with evidence it significantly reduces chronic anxiety, working at least as well as medication over long periods.[41 & 42] Regular exercise also has the benefit of providing long-lasting muscle relaxation, which, like the muscle relaxation exercises we outlined earlier, reduces muscle tension throughout the body and in turn dampens amygdala reactivity, further contributing to lower levels of anxiety.[43]

Physical Activity as Exposure Treatment

Exercise can also be particularly beneficial for people who struggle with panic attacks or the strong physiological symptoms of anxiety or stress. Moderate physical activity can act as a type of exposure treatment, helping us to get used to the physical sensations often experienced when anxious or stressed. Experiencing similar sensations while exercising (increased heart rate, rapid breathing, elevated blood pressure) helps us to realise they are not harmful. We learn to cope with them and get used to the discomfort.[44]

But I Don't Like Physical Activity

I've read and taught about the benefits of physical activity for a long time. I have noticed that despite growing evidence of the benefits of exercise and appeals to get more active from the media, health experts, and government campaigns, most people still don't exercise regularly. To be motivated to exercise, people must either enjoy what they are doing or make it a part of everyday life, whether through necessity or choice. My love of walking came from having to walk 25 minutes to the train station from my home and then another 20 minutes after getting off the train to my place of work every day. I probably would have driven to the train station if I'd had a car. However, four years of enforced walking turned into a habit I love, and I've long continued to walk every day despite no longer needing to do the same daily commute.

People often find physical activity challenging to start and maintain because it is seen as a chore. Exercise has become synonymous with going to the gym. While some people love visiting the gym, for many of us, the gym is a sterile, artificial, and intimidating environment that can be off-putting. The most important criteria for deciding what exercise you should do is enjoyment. If we enjoy what we do, we are more likely to keep doing it. Think about what exercise you can do outside the gym, whether at a club, at home, or outside.

Exercising outside – in nature – known as 'green exercise', has been shown to have extra mental health benefits above and beyond physical activity. These include improvements in mood and self-esteem and reductions in anxiety and depression.[45] I may be biased due to my love of walking, but having taught the benefits of exercise for many years, I am convinced that if there is a panacea in medicine, it is walking. If you do nothing else, walk for 10 to 20 minutes daily and slowly introduce more walking into your everyday life. The recommended dose is between 8,000 to 12,000 steps daily, about 3 to 5 miles. Get a pedometer or activity monitor to see how far you're walking. Build up to a level of fitness that allows you to walk briskly for some of the time.

Whatever exercise you do, try to do it with moderate intensity and make sure your doctor approves it. Consider incorporating it into *'Foundational Exercise 2: Balancing Life'* outlined in the *Calming the Mind* part of the book.

ASSESS YOUR MEDIA DIET

Our human negativity bias, a survival strategy inherited from our early ancestors who lived in dangerous environments, naturally draws our attention to negative news stories. This is why negative stories dominate the media, and we feel compelled to watch them. So, it's natural to want to follow updates on terrorist events, violence, shootings, and war, both on television and social media. However, repeated exposure to trauma by the media can have as similar an impact as experiencing the event first-hand.

How Constantly Consuming the News Can Increase Your Anxiety

You may think it is necessary to keep up with the news, and those who follow the media are more informed about the world's dangers, but this isn't the case. People who digest more media grossly overestimate rates of violence.[46] We can compound this and raise our levels of anxiety and helplessness further by reading fearful and angry public comments on what has happened and what action should be taken. Consuming the news this way makes us far more anxious and afraid because we don't tend to be very good at assessing risk. We overestimate our chances of being in danger due to a number of irrational ways of thinking. Some of them include:

- If a recent event is particularly dramatic and receives saturation coverage in the media, we tend to overestimate the risk of something similar happening to ourselves. We do not see dramatic, in-depth media coverage of other causes of death, which are more common, such as road traffic accidents, so we assume the events that receive more coverage are more dangerous to us.
- We lack awareness of the more common positive or neutral events. We don't focus on the far more common non-events that occur every day, such as the number of flights that safely arrive at an airport or the number of positive social interactions between people of different religions. These events, which are a far more accurate indicator of reality, do not make the news as they are common and are more likely to occur.
- We succumb to the recency effect. We think a dramatic event is more likely to happen if a similar event happened recently. This is the case after terrorist attacks, virus outbreaks such as Ebola, and aeroplane accidents.

Is the World Becoming Less Safe?

Although it sometimes feels like the world is becoming less safe, peaceful and united, and therefore more dangerous, violent, and divided, is this the case? If you look at the measurements objectively, the world we currently live in is probably more peaceful, safe, and less dangerous than at any other time.[47 & 48] Despite this, most of us have never felt as disturbed about the world before, so it feels as if things are worse.

What has changed is how we get our information; there are now far more cameras to record small and large incidents, an internet that helps us spread information more quickly and widely, and the far-reaching effects of social media. So, the type of information we now receive has changed, along with the way we get it.

We are living in an attention economy, and the information that gets the most attention is extremism and fear-mongering. As we've discussed before, our negativity bias naturally gravitates towards this type of information, even if it is unbalanced. So, extreme views are rewarded with more attention, shares, and comments. Social media, some news channels, and the internet in general have developed a medium in which moderate views, respectful discussion, and reasonable behaviour are considered boring and uninteresting.

Distraction and Cognitive Overload

Continual media exposure also distracts us from getting on with other activities we need to do or would benefit from and can also overload our thinking. Endless access to new information quickly overwhelms our working memory. When we reach cognitive overload, our ability to transfer learning to long-term memory significantly deteriorates. It's as if our brain has become a full cup of water, and anything more poured into it spills out. So we leave ourselves with little time to do other things properly and are also unable to focus as well on other information.

You may also notice that stopping can be difficult once you start looking at news and social media. It almost becomes an addiction. Our brain craves continual stimulation, is drawn to novelty, and likes to be instantly gratified. Continually watching or reading updates creates a compulsion loop, and like drug addicts, we need more and more 'hits' to get the same effect. Try to be aware of being caught up in a compulsion loop. Notice it when you can; you may be surprised by how mindlessly you do this.

News websites and social media apps aim to keep us viewing for as long and as often as possible. The design of the apps and websites, along with the algorithms that drive them and the notifications produced by them, have one aim - to make as much money as possible from our continued use. We are often manipulated by computer code written by people whose job is to keep us hooked. To make sure, in other words, that almost everything else you could be doing seems boring by comparison. For example, one way they achieve this is by the reinforcement trick of 'variable reward', ensuring that when you click, swipe or hit refresh, you're sometimes – but not always – rewarded with an update, email, like, etc. (If you always got the reward, you'd soon get bored.) Notice that when you open X (formerly known as Twitter), there's a tiny pause before you're told the number of notifications you receive. This is deliberately engineered, so you'll be on tenterhooks every time.

You can be held hostage to a news cycle whose primary aim is to make money from your fear, outrage, and mindless dependence on more of the same. We don't gain anything by consuming news constantly and would be just as informed if we checked less often. We get hit by wave after wave of 'breaking news' but never see the ocean.

As a personal example, I remember when I used to view social media very frequently. I sometimes found that when I closed my eyes at night, went in the shower, or did anything that didn't take up my full attention, my head would be full of the voices of those

I followed on social media. They were constantly swirling around my head. I'd be party to arguments between others that didn't concern me, engrossed in problems I could do nothing about, and overloaded with so much information I couldn't process it all. We can lose our language and our unique way of thinking. We are fed clichés and repeat them in our heads and conversations with others.

After a while, I realised that others' thoughts were robbing me of peace and not allowing my thoughts to come through. My head was full of well-meaning advice, angry views, outraged voices, stories of injustice, fear, grudges, research findings, funny quips, and many polarised opinions. Meanwhile, I realised my life was being lived through the lens of others.

How Should We Stay Informed?

I am not saying that we should never catch up on the news or engage in social media or that it always has a negative effect. The internet and social media have also been a vehicle for good and provide some people with a voice and positive connections they previously didn't have access to. However, we should raise awareness of how often we access certain types of media and reflect on how we feel after this exposure. We should consider what kind of news we digest and what sources we rely on. We have the power to decide.

Plan times when you want to catch up with the news rather than accessing it continually, and try to notice when you're automatically checking for updates without being aware of what you're doing. Particularly consider your exposure to social media and news in the morning. Waking up and being bombarded by anxious news at the beginning of the morning can set your mood and pattern of thinking for the rest of the day.

If, after reflection, you become aware your media diet is problematic and adds to your anxiety, consider how you might change how you consume the news and any other media, and incorporate it into *'Preparing to Change Exercise 2: Balancing Life.'*

What we do with our time and how that affects our energy levels and mood is crucial to our mental well-being. Our energy levels significantly impact how well we can handle our emotions, how prepared we feel for challenges, and how effectively we can perform many tasks and activities. So, it's vital these foundations are in place when we make changes to our lives.

Next, we will look at exercises that calm the mind and help us understand our thinking patterns more clearly. These exercises enable us to make better decisions and feel more rested and peaceful.

TEN

Calming the Mind

E arlier in the book, we discussed the two routes to social anxiety.

1. The reactive route, which is amygdala-based.
2. The thought route, which is cortex-based.

The exercises in this chapter are beneficial for both routes and will prepare you for the mindfulness skills that will be introduced in the *Three Key Skills: Dealing with Anxious Thoughts and Feelings* part of the book. They have also been designed to build on the foundational exercises included in the previous chapters. First, they raise awareness of our thought patterns, giving us a clearer understanding of who we are. Second, they calm the mind and help manage energy levels.

MINDFULNESS

I'm sure many of you have heard of mindfulness before. Indeed, you may have even rolled your eyes when you first glanced at this subtitle. I certainly would have done so a few years back. One of the most popular mindfulness practices — meditation — has become increasingly popular in the Western world over the last ten years. Its benefits have been championed in many areas of life, from business and leadership settings to education and mental health. The blanket coverage of meditation and its perceived links with spirituality, religion, and later business performance put me off trying it for a long time. Furthermore, nearly every time I heard a talk about meditation or listened to a guided meditation, it was nearly always accompanied by panpipes in the background. I felt it wasn't for me.

However, after years of researching mental health treatments and interventions for my university health psychology class, I was won over by the science. I understood that meditation and several other mindfulness practices are very effective mental training methods.

While meditation is an excellent mindfulness practice, as Dan Siegel outlines in his book *The Mindful Brain*, other simple forms of mindfulness can be just as effective.[49] Mindfulness is the simple process of actively noticing new things. When you notice something, it puts you in the present, whether it's observing the thoughts in your head, the breath entering in and out of your nostrils, the softness of the jumper you're wearing, the tone of someone else's voice, or the shapes of buildings in the distance. In the exercises in this chapter, we will focus on meditation as it provides a structure and routine for mindfulness that many find helpful, especially when first practising.

We mentioned experience-dependent neuroplasticity earlier, explaining that we now see the brain as more like a muscle that can be changed with exercise and that what we do with our attention matters. Our brains are plastic, meaning neurons can change how they interact with experience, and neural pathways can be strengthened or weakened depending on how much they are used. Whenever we engage in repeated behaviour, it can lead to changes in our brain structure. For example, studies show if you practise juggling, you'll increase the grey matter in the areas of your brain associated with visual motion.[50]

While we are just beginning to understand neuroplasticity, a growing body of evidence shows that mindfulness practices can benefit brain function and structure. Let's examine these changes a little more closely.

BRAIN FUNCTION

Neurobiological research on mindfulness practices has testified to various changes in brain functioning – how well the brain performs specific tasks. Some of the most prominent changes have been documented in three areas: attention, age-related cognitive decline, and emotional control.

Attention

Control over where we direct our attention is vital to managing our emotions and behaviour. Research has demonstrated many improvements in brain function in various types of attention.[51]

- These include improvements in **alerting** — becoming aware of a stimulus — like an alarm sounding.
- Positive changes have also been discovered in **sustained attention** — our ability to follow a stimulus over time — such as focusing for an extended period on a task that needs to be completed.
- Improvements have also been found in **conflict monitoring** — remaining focused despite distractions trying to pull our attention away — such as continuing to concentrate on a conversation despite being tempted to check phone notifications.

Age-Related Cognitive Decline

The practices have also been shown to stave off and slow down normal age-related cognitive decline in the areas of:[52]

- **Short-term memory**: Our capacity for remembering information in an active, readily available state for a short period. For example, remembering the drinks of everyone in your group while making an order at the bar.
- **Perceptual speed**: The ability to process information quickly and accurately, particularly under time pressure. It includes how quickly and accurately we can recognise and compare numbers, letters, objects, pictures, or patterns.
- **Executive functioning**: A mix of cognitive skills, including the mental processes that enable us to plan, focus, remember instructions, and multitask successfully. We use executive functioning to filter distractions, prioritise tasks, set and achieve goals, and control impulses.

Emotional Control

Finally, research has shown meditative practices can help us to take charge of our emotions by:

- **Dampening amygdala activation** both in the short-term and long-term, making anxious responses less reactive.[53]
- **Reducing the fight, flight or freeze response** by activating the parasympathetic nervous system. This calms down anxious thinking and reduces the physiological anxiety response in the body.[54]

So, mindfulness practices can have an immediate impact and a long-term cumulative effect on anxiety. They also raise awareness of the chattering cortex, making them excellent foundational exercises.

BRAIN STRUCTURE

There have also been several research studies by Sara Lazar and her Harvard University colleagues documenting how mindfulness practices change the physical structure of the brain.[55]

- Ageing is usually related to **cortical thinning** - losing grey matter in the prefrontal cortex. This is why, as we get older, it's more challenging to work out complex problems and remember things. Losing grey matter when we age is normal. Still, compared to people of the same age, studies have shown that people who meditate have thicker anterior insulae, sensory cortices, and prefrontal cortices. Fifty-year-old meditators have been shown to have the same amount of grey matter as twenty-five-year-olds. These three regions are also all thought to be involved with integrating emotional and cognitive processes, so they help us manage and understand our emotions more effectively and improve the quality of our thinking. The opposite development — decreased volume of grey matter — has been associated with several clinical disorders, including social anxiety, post-traumatic stress disorder, specific phobias, and schizophrenia.
- Changes have also been demonstrated in the **hippocampus**, an area of the brain involved in learning, memory, and emotion regulation. Studies have shown that participants who completed an eight-week

mindfulness course increased grey matter concentration within the left hippocampus. Conversely, it shrinks in people who suffer from depression and anxiety, and stress also appears to shrink it.

- Research has revealed positive changes in an area of the brain called the **temporo-parietal junction**, which is located just above the ear. This area involves perspective taking, empathy, and compassion.
- Finally, changes have also been found in our friend, the amygdala, but studies show a decrease in grey matter for those practising mindfulness. During an eight-week mindfulness programme, the more stress reduction reported, the smaller the amygdala.

MEDITATION

When done consistently, mindfulness practices, including meditation, can help us manage our emotions, alter brain structure and function, and positively change our behaviour. Despite these benefits, many people are still put off from starting meditation or find it difficult to continue with the practice after a few attempts. Let's look at some difficulties or blocks people encounter when attempting to start or continue with meditation.

1. **Some people are deterred by meditation's spiritual or religious connotations** (and mindfulness in general), but need not be. While some religious or spiritual people meditate, meditation is not a religion; many atheists and agnostics also meditate. Meditation doesn't have to be a religious practice, and the meditations included in this book are written as mental training exercises.

2. **Many people think meditation takes up a lot of time**, but this isn't necessarily the case. You may have read stories of Tibetan monks meditating for up to 16 hours a

day, but the research shows a daily practice from any time between two to twenty minutes can positively impact mental well-being. You have to be patient and persistent to reap the benefits, but you will also find that the practice brings a clear-headedness and peace that can help you spend the time you have more effectively.

3. **People often remark that they cannot meditate because their minds are too busy, or they find it nearly impossible not to think**. Meditation isn't about 'not thinking' or emptying your head of thoughts. This is the misconception I hear most often. It's about training your brain to focus its attention on one thing. People frequently say they can't do that; they find it impossible, but it comes with practice. It was a revelation for me to learn that the act of bringing your attention back to the thing you're focusing on (e.g. the breath) is the practice of meditation itself. Just like continually lifting a weight will build muscle in an arm, consistently bringing your attention back to the point of focus will build the ability to meditate. So when the mind wanders, the meditation isn't a failure. Our brain is like a wayward puppy, out of control. Catching it and returning it to the object of focus is the mediation.

4. **Some people fear that by meditating, they will lose their edge and** drive to succeed; they will be too calm, relaxed, and brimming with peace to be effective in life. It's not about that at all. It's about understanding how your mind works—the thinking patterns you get caught up in—and then training your attention to be more focused when needed. This helps us see situations more clearly and take wiser action.

5. **Finally, having been bombarded by magazine photos and YouTube clips of an archetypical meditation pose, people believe in meditating, they need to be sitting**

cross-legged on a cushion, palms of their hands facing the sky, wearing yoga pants, with a small column of meditation stones by their side. It's true; some people find it more comfortable to sit cross-legged on a cushion, and if that works for you, that's great. However, many meditate seated on a chair or standing up if needed. You can meditate on public transport and even when walking. There will be more advice on what to do with your body when you meditate within the details of the specific exercises.

∼

Calming the Mind Exercise 1:
Mindfulness Meditation

One of the most effective ways to start meditating is to focus on something that is always with us—our breath. For this exercise, follow the instructions on the audio recording using the link further down the page.

I suggest you practise this meditation once daily, intending to do it most days. You can do it using a posture that is comfortable for you, but you should aim to be alert and not sleepy. Feel free to use a chair or sit on a cushion, but aim to adopt an erect and dignified posture if your environment allows you to. When I first meditated, I would often lie down on my bed or the floor, but I fell asleep more often than not. You can choose any time of the day to meditate, whichever suits you best. Many people find meditating first thing in the morning sets them up nicely for the rest of the day, but any time of the day will be beneficial.

You can find an audio recording of the guided meditation here: https://soundcloud.com/dr-matt-lewis

You can listen to it on your computer, phone, tablet, or other device. Start with the 10-minute exercise and then try longer meditations when ready. It's best to start with shorter meditations to help you become confident with the practice, make it easier to commit to it and build a habit. However, stick with the ten-minute meditation if you feel ten minutes suits you.

As time goes by and you get used to the format of the meditation, you might feel you don't need to use the recording. You will soon realise that the meditation process is simple, and you can fit it into your life more spontaneously — when you have the time and space to do so — even if you're on public transport or sitting on a park bench. With some experience, you can design your meditations to fit any time frame, from as short as one minute upwards. The general structure of mindfulness meditation is as follows:

- **Intention**: Start by creating an intention for your meditation. It may be to reduce your anxiety, lower your stress, or be calmer throughout the day. Every time you make an intention, you're forming or reinforcing a mental habit, and this action alone can guide your behaviour and positively impact your decision-making.

- **Follow your breath**: Gently bring your attention to your breathing. People do this in many different ways, such as focusing on the breath entering and leaving the nostrils or noticing the rising and falling of the chest.

- **Distraction**: You may find yourself in a state where your mind is calm and concentrated, gently following the breath, but sooner or later, you will find yourself falling into distraction, worrying, or fantasising (much sooner rather than later when you first meditate). This is normal. After a while, you will notice that your attention has wandered, and most people, especially beginners, react to this realisation with self-criticism, telling themselves they're terrible meditators. At this point, you should:

- **Bring your attention back to the breath**: Remember, noticing your attention has wandered and then bringing it back to the breath is the process of meditation itself. This is not a failure; it is what it is all about. So you should try to do this with kindness to yourself and an attitude of curiosity.

Can't Do Ten Minutes of Meditation?

Some people find it challenging to start with even ten minutes of meditation. We are so used to our attention being pulled in different directions that ten minutes can seem like a lifetime when attempting meditation for the first time.

So, how do you make the practice of meditation as easy to start as possible and so compelling it is self-sustaining? **If you find ten minutes an impossible starting point, I'd suggest that you plan to do less than you are sure you can comfortably manage.** For example, if you can sit and meditate for five minutes, don't meditate for this long; do two to three minutes. Aim to do this a few times daily instead of one longer session. If you can only do two minutes, aim only to do one minute. If one minute is as much as you can manage, aim for 30 seconds.

You're doing this to avoid meditation becoming burdensome. If it feels like a chore, you won't be able to sustain it. So sit often but for short periods. You'll likely enjoy and look forward to those sessions and want to make those sessions longer as time goes by.

What if you can't even do thirty seconds? If, when you're honest with yourself, even half a minute of meditation feels like a burden, commit to one mindful breath a day. This commitment should be easy to fulfil and give you momentum. When you are ready for more, it will be easy to expand it, even if it's just two breaths a day. Also, just making this intention is a form of mindfulness and will develop a valuable mental habit that will grow and expand over time.

If you enjoy walking or need to walk often as a part of your everyday routine, you may find it easier to do a walking meditation. It has the same focus and rigour as sitting meditation. It can also help during anxious times when the physiological reactions occurring in the body make it difficult to sit still. Don't worry. A walking meditation doesn't involve closing your eyes or any cushion carrying — it's about where and how you focus your attention when you're out and about.

Calming the Mind Exercise 2: Walking Meditation

Walking meditation is simple; it involves bringing moment-to-moment attention to the movements of your walking, and every time your attention wanders away, bring it back to those movements. To help you start, there is a guided walking meditation you can stream or download and listen to as you walk here:

https://soundcloud.com/dr-matt-lewis/walking-meditation

If you find it challenging to carve out enough time for the formal sitting or walking meditation exercises, you can still incorporate mindfulness into other areas of your life, just as you're going about your everyday routines. Even if you can find time for the formal practices, you can extend their benefits by practising mindfulness in this way. You can train yourself to focus your attention on whatever you are doing, whether it be walking, running, drawing, making a hot drink, or sitting down.

So, when you usually reach for your smartphone to waste a few moments, such as when you're waiting in line, focus on your breath for a few moments instead. Of course, it wouldn't be beneficial or practical for you to do everything mindfully, but you can inject some mindfulness into your day by focusing on whatever you are doing and consistently bringing your attention back to the activity whenever your mind wanders.

Calming the Mind Exercise 3: Routine Tasks

This exercise helps us be awake for a few more moments each day and avoid being on autopilot when doing a routine everyday activity. Choose one of the following activities or one of your choosing, and try to pay attention when doing it. You can choose different activities on different days or stick to one activity if you find it particularly helpful.

When you choose an activity, go at your own pace. You don't have to slow it down or even enjoy it, but see if you can be fully alive and aware of your actions as you do it. When your attention wanders, as it will, just gently bring it back to the task, focusing on all the actions and physical sensations of the task.

- Walking from one room to another
- Cleaning a surface in the kitchen
- Brushing your teeth
- Taking a shower
- Getting dressed or undressed
- Drinking tea, coffee, water, or juice
- Doing the dishes or filling the dishwasher

- Taking out the rubbish (trash)
- Loading the washing machine or tumble drier
- Waiting in a queue (look at people and objects around you, listen to the different sounds, etc.)
- Waiting at traffic lights (whilst still being aware of the colour of the lights, notice the sights and sounds around you).

PART III
Three Key Skills:

DEALING WITH ANXIOUS THOUGHTS AND
FEELINGS

ELEVEN

Effectively Managing Anxious Thoughts

DEFUSION

We discussed the Acceptance and Commitment Therapy (ACT) mindfulness skills of defusion, expansion, and engagement earlier in Chapter 5, explaining they can help us manage our anxious thinking. This section of the book includes three short chapters, one on each of these ACT skills.

The best way to understand and learn these skills is to try them out yourself. While they may seem slightly contrived initially, they become easy to implement after some practice. Soon, you will find you can do them intuitively and with little effort. The skills work particularly well for people who struggle with social anxiety, helping us to stop focusing on social danger and giving us the skills to move from safety mode to action mode.

In Chapter 5, we also discussed the two routes to anxiety and said our cortex can initiate anxiety in one of two ways:

- Interpreting neutral sensory information as dangerous and sending this information to the amygdala to produce anxiety.
- Independently creating anxious thoughts and feelings without sensory information and, again, sending this information to the amygdala to produce anxiety.

We can learn to manage these unhelpful thoughts with practice and stop or significantly reduce the amygdala's reaction. This allows us to take control of our behaviour and engage fully with our actions instead of avoiding uncomfortable situations. We will now learn how to put the skills into practice, focusing firstly on defusion.

UNDERSTANDING DEFUSION

At the heart of defusion are words and images. We use words in different contexts:

- Words we read are called text.
- Words we speak out loud are called speech.
- Words inside our heads are called thoughts.

The thoughts inside our heads can also be images: still images like photographs or moving images like film clips. We often forget our thoughts are just words or images that we turn into stories. These stories can be true (facts) or false (lies), but they are usually based on how we see life through our experiences, opinions, judgements, and morals. They are about what we have done in the past or what we want, expect, or fear in the future.

I want to clarify that thinking is essential, and this book is not against it! Thinking allows us to learn from the past and plan for the future. These are vital human skills that we need to survive and thrive, but sometimes, we can get too caught up in our thoughts and stories, and when they are unhelpful, this can lead to difficulties. An unhelpful thought or story can dominate our mind, take our full attention and dictate our behaviour. This is called 'fusion' — the act of getting caught up in our thoughts and considering them to be absolutely true.

> **Fusion:** When an unhelpful thought or story dominates our mind, takes up our full attention and dictates our behaviour.

To counteract unhelpful thoughts and stories, we can defuse or separate from them—become aware they are just thoughts. When we defuse our thoughts, we put the brakes on unhelpful thinking. We create for ourselves a small gap of awareness that allows us to stop or significantly reduce anxious thoughts and the resultant anxiety response.

> **Defusion**: When we create a small gap of awareness in our thinking that allows us to stop or significantly reduce the unhelpful thoughts and resultant anxiety response.

There are several ways we can defuse our thoughts, and in time and with practice, it is something we can learn to do automatically when needed. I'd recommend you try all the following defusion exercises and see which ones work best for you. Remember, one of the critical components of safety mode is fusing with anxious thoughts, both before and during social situations.

This first exercise illustrates how defusion works, but it can also be used as a practice to defuse unhelpful thoughts and stories.

Defusion Exercise 1: I Notice I'm Having the Thought

Step 1: Bring to mind a negative thought you have about social situations, one you have often. Maybe it's, *"I'm a loser, no one will want to talk to me'*, *'No one likes me'*, or *'I look awkward and ridiculous'*. Thought of one?

Step 2: Now, take a moment to 'Fuse' with that thought. Believe it as much as you can.

Step 3: Now insert this phrase in front of that thought…*"I'm having the thought that…"*

For example, *'I'm having the thought that...I'm a loser. No one will want to talk to me.'*

Step 4: Next, insert an extra phrase in front of that phrase…"*I notice that I'm having the thought that…*"

For example, *'I notice that I'm having the thought that...I'm a loser. No one will want to talk to me.'*

Can you feel the thought lose some of its impact?

You'll notice in this exercise that you weren't battling or disputing the thought; you were accepting it but not letting it influence you. When we defuse our thoughts like this, we realise thoughts are nothing more or less than words or pictures, and we can let them chatter away without obeying them. Negative thoughts are normal, so don't fight them; defuse them. You can use this defusion exercise to deal with anxious thoughts that may cause you to avoid a social situation or while experiencing anxious thoughts in the middle of a social situation.

THE POWER OF STORIES

The second defusion technique targets the power of stories. The mind loves stories, but unfortunately, many are unhelpful and negative, such as 'I can't do it', 'My life is terrible', or 'I'm boring'. Research shows that about eighty per cent of our thoughts have negative content, but negative stories aren't the problem. The problem is getting caught up in them and letting them dictate our actions.

When our mind tells us an unhelpful story, we usually try to **change it** (by arguing in our head, *'No, I'm not stupid, I'm capable,*

I've achieved things. I have!"), **distract ourselves from it** (watch TV, surf the web, eat something nice), or **blank it out** in some way (sleep, food, alcohol, drugs). Trying to change, avoid, or get rid of the story is often ineffective, time-consuming, and focuses our attention on the unhelpful story. It may work briefly, but the thought nearly always comes back later. Instead, name a story for what it is — a story.

As a personal example, when considering doing social things outside of my comfort zone, my mind would often respond with, *'Don't be stupid. You stupid idiot, Matt.'* These thoughts would come automatically in a split second, and I'd find myself arguing or distracting myself from the thoughts by humming loudly (yes, really!). As a result, I'd often cancel social plans or arrive low in confidence and find a corner to hide in. When I learned about defusion, I called this the *'Matt is Stupid'* story. The stories start to lose their impact when we name them. We begin to realise they are just stories.

Defusion Exercise 2: The Power of Stories

Step 1: Notice when your mind starts telling you a familiar story. It may not always use the exact same thoughts or images each time, but there will be a pattern of thinking or a narrative you recognise.

Step 2: Name the story (silently in your head). Ah! There it is again, the — *'I'm a Loser'* story, *'I'll look stupid', 'I can't cope'* story, *'I'm unlovable'* story, *'Not good enough'* story. Give it any name you want.

Step 3: Continue to name the story every time you notice it, but try to do it with warmth and, if appropriate, humour.

So when an unhelpful thought or story comes, we need to notice it, name it, and neutralise it. Although this may seem like a simple strategy, you are training your cortex to be aware of your sticky thoughts and thinking patterns, and in time, you will start to see the stories lose their impact on your behaviour.

Defusion Exercise 3: Thanking the Mind

The third defusion technique is simple, quick, and effective, and it's the one I find most helpful. When your mind comes up with those same old stories or unhelpful thoughts, simply thank it.

Say (silently to yourself), *'Thanks, mind!'*, *'Thanks for sharing!'*, *'Is that right?'*, *'That's amazing!'*, *'That's so informative!'* Don't do this sarcastically or aggressively, but do it with warmth, humour, and genuine appreciation for the incredible storytelling ability of your mind. This simple act of noticing and acknowledging the thoughts or stories will start to reduce their power.

Some people like to give their mind a name when they thank it. They find that the name creates a slightly more significant gap in awareness. For example, *'Thanks for the thought, George, thanks for sharing!'*

IMAGES AND MOVING PICTURES

If your unhelpful thoughts appear as images or video-style film clips of memories and predictions of what could happen, there are several strategies you can use to defuse them. The methods are very similar to the previous ones, providing a gap of awareness that allows you to step back and observe your thoughts before taking action.

Defusion Exercise 4: Lights, Camera, Action!

Step 1: When an unhelpful image or video clip pops into your head, imagine a television near you and put the image or video on the television.

Step 2: Now, play around with the image. Turn it upside down, flip it around, stretch it, play the video backwards, and turn the colour and brightness up and down. There are lots of ways you can play with it. Give it subtitles and a soundtrack, or put it in different locations. It doesn't have to be a television — you can put the image on a computer screen, poster, or t-shirt — be creative and see what works best for you.

Remember, the aim isn't to eliminate unpleasant images but to see them for what they are — just pictures.

HELP WITH DEFUSION

Try out some of these exercises when you're having unhelpful thoughts or imagining unpleasant images, and see which ones work best for you. Don't expect miraculous overnight changes — although possible — it usually takes practice, but you will see progress sooner rather than later. When you first practise defusion, notice your experience without judging yourself; rather than being critical, be curious about it. With persistence, you will eventually notice being aware of unhelpful thoughts and defusing them becomes second nature, and in time, you'll be able to do it without using any techniques.

WHAT IF MY THOUGHTS ARE TRUE?

When first hearing about defusion, people often respond by asking, *'But what if the thoughts are true?'* Your thoughts may be true, but a more important question is: *'Are my thoughts helpful?'*

So, for example, if you are asked to do a presentation for a job, you may think, *'I'm incompetent; I'll never be able to do this'*. It may be true that you do not have the skills to do that task then, but does holding that thought encourage you to look after yourself or take action? For some people, that type of thought might motivate them and spur them into action. If it does, that's fine. Fuse with it. However, most people would find a thought like that blaming and demoralising, and it doesn't encourage them to look after themselves or to take action. It would be unhelpful.

An example of a more helpful thought that could come, one that may be better to fuse with or hold on to, is 'I can ask for help' or 'With practice, *I will get better'*. Most people would consider that to be an encouraging thought, one that could lead to helpful behaviour. Remember, you're not replacing one thought with another; you're noticing what an unhelpful thought is and what a helpful thought is, and you're deciding whether to hold onto and fuse with that thought or defuse it. So what's important is not whether a thought is true but whether holding onto that thought helps you to take care of yourself and take positive action.

THE MAIN PURPOSE OF DEFUSION

People often get the wrong idea about defusion, thinking it's a clever way to get rid of negative thoughts. This is because, usually, when we defuse a thought, it disappears and, over time, shows up less. However, consider this a lucky bonus, a by-product of defusion. It may not always happen and is not the primary purpose of defusion. The main purpose of defusion is to be present and to be able to take effective action. Defusion isn't about battling with, blocking, distracting from, or getting rid of thoughts, but accepting and defusing them.

Now that we've learned how to handle thoughts and images, the next chapter will explain how to deal with unpleasant and uncomfortable feelings.

TWELVE

Accepting Anxious Feelings

EXPANSION

W hen social anxiety causes us to experience painful or uncomfortable feelings, emotions, and sensations, we usually do our best to avoid them, distract ourselves from them, or try to get rid of them. When we do this, we can often find relief in the short term, but it makes our lives more difficult in the long term. We can learn to deal with these feelings effectively by learning a skill called 'expansion'.

In ACT, the term 'expansion' is really another name for **acceptance**. We're using the term expansion because most people misunderstand acceptance as wanting, tolerating, liking, or putting up with.

Expansion can be described as the ability to open up and make room for emotions, sensations, and feelings. Allowing them to come and go without letting them drag us down, push us around, or hold us back. It's a powerful way to handle difficult emotions such as fear, anger and anxiety.

So, rather than trying to get rid of unpleasant feelings, we open up and accommodate them. We make room and allow them to come and go in their own good time. This doesn't mean we want them, like them, or approve of them, but we stop investing our time and effort in fighting them. The more space we can give difficult feelings, the smaller their influence and impact on our lives.

The following exercise illustrates how expansion works but can also be used to practise expansion when experiencing uncomfortable emotions, feelings, or sensations.

Expansion Exercise: N.A.M.E: (Notice, Acknowledge, Make Space, Expand Awareness)

Step 1: Think of a social situation that makes you mildly anxious. Nothing too extreme, just something that gives you some mild to moderate anxious feelings, whether it's making a speech, having to order something at a busy bar (one of mine), or walking into a room of strangers. Maybe it's a real up-and-coming social task you need to do that you're not looking forward to. Take a little time to think of something.

Step 2: Observe. Now, observe the sensations in your body. Just thinking about that situation should bring about some feelings in your body. Just observe those sensations. Where are they in your body? There may be more than one sensation. If so, look for the one that bothers you the most. Be curious about it. Where does it start and stop? What shape do you imagine it to be? Is it light or heavy? Is it moving or staying still? Is it warm or cool?

Step 3: Breathe. Now, breathe into and around the sensation. Slow, deep breaths if you can. Deep breaths can lower the tension in your body, increase your vagal tone, and help you to switch from the sympathetic nervous system (fight or flight and aggressive) to the parasympathetic nervous system (calmer and restful). This won't eliminate your feelings but will provide some calmness within you, like an anchor in the storm. Imagine your breath flowing into and around the sensation.

Step 4: Make space. As your breath flows in and around the sensation, imagine it's creating extra space within your body, so you're giving it plenty of room to move. If the feeling gets bigger, give it even more space and allow it even more room.

Step 5: Allow. Now allow that sensation to be there, even though you may not like it or want it. Just let it be there. If your mind comments on what's happening, thank it and return to observing. You may feel an urge to fight it or push it away. If so, acknowledge that urge and return your attention to the sensation or feeling. Remember, you're not trying to get rid of or change it, but if it changes by itself, that's fine. Keep observing it until you completely give up the struggle with it and accept it.

Step 6: Expand awareness. When you've given up the struggle with the sensation, expand your awareness to the present moment, whatever is happening right now. What is happening in the room you're in? What can you see, hear, smell? Think of it as bringing the lights up on a stage. Typically, when we're anxious, we have a spotlight that focuses only on the anxious feeling. Now, however, you've acknowledged the sensation, and you're bringing up the lights and taking in your environment.

I always found it difficult to order drinks at a bar, and the busier the bar, the worse I felt. As I approached a bar, my breathing would increase, my heartbeat would rise, and my stomach would churn. For a long time, I tried to avoid the situation by not going to bars with my friends or by excusing myself by visiting the toilet when it was my turn to get some drinks and handing money to a friend to go to the bar for me.

Now, I don't avoid the situation. I allow the feelings to be there, give them some room, and let them come and go in their own time. I don't allow my feelings to dictate my actions, shrink my life, or control my behaviour. Over time, it has gotten much easier, and often, I don't feel anxious at all, but if I do, I practise expansion. With practice, the six steps have become intuitive, and I implement them within seconds.

Take the example of a job interview. Just before entering the room, you may start to feel anxious. This is perfectly normal. Rather than leaving the situation, arguing with your feelings, or telling yourself to calm down, you can notice the anxiety, give it space, and allow it to come and go while 'bringing up the lights' on your environment. This will enable you to engage with the present moment – the people in the room and the questions you're being asked. The anxiety may still be there, but it is not controlling your behaviour.

This should give you a taste of what expansion is like. At times, you may experience lots of sensations, and if this is the case, go through them one after the other, using the technique until you stop struggling. With practice, you'll learn to do this naturally and quickly — you'll notice an uncomfortable emotion or feeling, and rather than trying to control it or allow it to control you, you'll accept it and give it space, allowing it to come and go while being able to engage in the present moment.

Like defusion, people often get the wrong idea about expansion, presuming it's just a clever way to eliminate uncomfortable or painful feelings. This is understandable, as when we use expansion, the uncomfortable feelings often disappear and, over time, show up less. However, don't expect this each time. Consider it a lucky bonus, a by-product of expansion, not the primary purpose. The main aim of expansion is to reduce the influence and impact of difficult feelings for us to be present and take effective action.

THIRTEEN

Being Present in Social Situations

ENGAGEMENT

So far in this section, we've talked about defusion: accepting unhelpful thoughts but reducing or eliminating their impact on us. This is followed by expansion: accepting uncomfortable feelings, letting them come and go, but not allowing them to influence us. The next step is engaging with experiences, tasks, and situations, despite unhelpful thoughts and uncomfortable feelings —staying present and engaging with life.

Engagement is being present instead of caught up in our thoughts and feelings. It is about being fully in the moment, open to, curious about, and actively involved in our here-and-now experience. Being able to be engaged and present is essential if we need to perform well in challenging situations or if we want to find satisfaction and fulfilment in whatever we are doing.

If we want to do anything well, perform confidently at an interview, talk to strangers, make a presentation, or learn a difficult skill, we must be engaged in what is happening. Being anxious or having negative thoughts about doing something is normal and not the problem. The problem is being caught up, lost in these thoughts, and disengaged from our experience. The more we focus on the unhelpful thoughts and feelings, the more we disconnect from the present moment. If we are continually inside our head, we're paralysed, unable to take action, or if we do, it's in a distracted and less effective way.

This particularly tends to happen when we experience social anxiety. We get hooked on stories about the future, how things might go wrong and how badly we'll handle them. This stops us from doing things and makes us even more anxious in the long run. It's a vicious circle. If a person feels lonely because they are anxious about socialising with others, they may often stay home instead of meeting with friends. This may relieve their anxiety but makes the situation worse over time — they become lonelier. To live fully, we must practise engaging with the present moment despite feeling anxious.

We don't always have to be connected to the present moment. It's okay to be lost in our thoughts sometimes. However, it is beneficial to be present in many situations. This includes activities we find pleasant or nourishing. We want to be engaged in these activities rather than lost in anxiety or worry. Likewise, there are activities, tasks, or situations that we may not find pleasant — talking to a group of people, attending a medical appointment, making a difficult phone call — but we need to engage with them to get what we want out of life, to protect ourselves, and to open doors to opportunities we might otherwise miss. Practising engagement allows us to be fully present when we need to.

Engagement, or fully paying attention to something, is also a clever way to silence negative thoughts, as it deliberately over-loads our attentional bandwidth. For example, when feeling angry, we can focus on something in such a way that anger isn't an option. Try ranting while also being engrossed in a crossword puzzle. It's impossible. You can also do the same with anxiety. The key is to pause, be aware of the stories inside your head, use defu-sion, allow any uncomfortable feelings to come and go in their own time, and then engage or focus fully on the task.

Let's go through some exercises that will allow us to practise engagement. When we're feeling anxious and need to engage in a task, activity, or situation, we will then be able to focus our attention on our environment and the present moment. Increasing our ability to focus our attention is a skill that can be learned, and the more we practise, the easier it will be. We can then transfer the engagement skills to situations that make us anxious.

Engagement Exercise: Engaging with Activities

Engaging with a Neutral Activity: In the '*Calming the Mind*' chapter, we introduced an exercise encouraging staying present when completing routine tasks (Calming the Mind Exercise 3). This should have given you a taste of practising engaging with the present moment while doing a neutral task.

Pick a task or activity you feel neutral about (you find it neither pleasant nor unpleasant) and engage with it fully, focusing carefully on all the actions and physical sensations of the task. If your mind wanders, bring your attention back to the activity and be present with what you are doing.

Engaging with a Pleasant Activity: Now practise engagement — being fully present — when doing a pleasant activity. This should be something you enjoy. It will differ from individual to individual. It may involve eating a nice lunch, walking your dog, reading a book, doing a Sudoku puzzle, listening to birds, sitting in the sunshine, or having a hug. You decide. Connect or engage with the task fully through the five senses, defusing your thoughts and making room for your feelings. If your mind wanders, bring your attention back to the task.

Engaging with a Task You Have Been Avoiding: Using the same principles as above, stay present when doing an activity or task you have been avoiding—something you may have been putting off for a while. It may be because it's unpleasant, boring, disagreeable, or makes you anxious. Connect or engage with the task fully through the five senses, defusing your thoughts and making room for your feelings. If your mind wanders, bring your attention back to the task.

These exercises help us practise being engaged with the present moment—whether it's neutral, pleasant, or unpleasant—so we can do so when necessary. Later in the book, we'll use engagement to stay present in social situations that create anxiety, but for now, the focus is on building up the 'engagement muscle'.

It's important to note we don't have to be present or engaged with absolutely everything we do all the time. Thinking of something else when doing an activity or task may be beneficial. It's okay to plan what we will do with our evening when washing the dishes or cleaning the floor. The problem is when our anxious feelings drive unhelpful behaviour, or when we avoid activities we need to do, perform poorly at a task we want to do well in, or are not benefitting from being present in a pleasurable activity that will nourish us.

In the next section, we will combine the skills we have learned so far and practically apply them. We'll use them to overcome fear, take action when it really matters, and be confident in social situations.

PART IV
Action Mode

A STEP-BY-STEP SOCIAL ANXIETY PLAN

FOURTEEN

Exposure Treatment

CONFRONTING SOCIAL ANXIETY

Now that we've learned the mindfulness skills of defusion, expansion, and engagement, it's time to put them into practice. This isn't easy, but it is possible and often life-changing. When we see anxiety-inducing situations as opportunities to learn, improve, and grow, we adopt a mindset of courage and optimism. Initial successes will boost our confidence, and future challenges won't seem insurmountable.

Taking practical steps to overcome social anxiety can be demanding at first. This is because once specific social anxiety triggers are established and a neural pattern has been formed; it's difficult to stop the amygdala from flooding us with anxiety. However, with practice, we can retrain the brain's response to anxiety and develop new pathways that compete with and over-power the original anxiety response. To do this, we need to expose ourselves to those very situations that trigger our anxiety and then counter the association between the trigger and negative social events or situations.

The defusion and expansion skills will help us to effectively manage our unhelpful thoughts and feelings when we confront our anxiety, and engagement will help to keep us present in the situation. This will allow our amygdala to learn from the new experience and make new connections in response to it.

In our everyday lives, there are many examples of people confronting and overcoming their anxiety in this way, and you've probably done it in other areas of your life before. Learning to drive and swim requires us to overcome some initial anxiety and ask anyone who's skied or parachuted if they had any anxiety when they first attempted it. We take many of these situations for granted and forget that we ever felt anxious. We can overcome unnecessary anxiety that stops us from living life fully in almost any situation and at any age.

By repeated exposure to an anxious situation - without anything negative happening - we can demonstrate to the amygdala that it doesn't require a fear response. We can teach our amygdala to feel safe.

You may remember discussing exposure treatment earlier in Chapter 6 when we described how psychologists typically treat *Escape Avoidance Learning* (the tendency to escape from anxious situations). It's been used to successfully treat panic attacks, obsessive-compulsive disorder (OCD), various phobias, and many anxiety-related disorders. Exposure treatment involves people being exposed to situations that make them fearful or anxious. Sometimes in gradual stages (like the example we used of the people treated for snake phobias) or sometimes abruptly.[56]

The treatment requires people to be exposed to the threatening situation, often causing their anxiety to rise to uncomfortable levels until eventually subsiding without them leaving the situation. Allowing the anxiety response to run its course without the person escaping is essential. This teaches the amygdala that similar situations are safe and shouldn't be feared.

For exposure treatment to work, we have to allow the amygdala to make new connections in the social situations that set off the anxiety response. This involves confronting our fears, which require courage and determination. We need to provoke the anxiety response, as only this activates the memory circuits that relate to that particular threatening situation, allowing new connections to be made and the amygdala to respond differently. This is why adopting the mindset that threats are an opportunity to learn and implement positive change is crucial. Exposure treatment isn't easy because it involves deliberately engaging in situations that we find anxiety-inducing.

TYPES OF EXPOSURE TREATMENT

The **gradual approach** is called **Systematic Desensitization** and involves gradually experiencing feared situations or objects. The treatment for snake phobias we discussed earlier in the book is an excellent example of the gradual approach. You may remember that the snake was introduced slowly but steadily, moving closer and closer, first from room to room and then within the room itself, allowing the person's anxiety to rise and fall before proceeding to the next stage.

The more **abrupt version** of the exposure treatment is called **Flooding**, and while it is a far more intense approach, it tends to provide relief from anxiety much more quickly. Rather than gradually building up to the fearful situation or object, people are thrown straight into the most anxiety-inducing situation and asked to stay with it until the anxiety subsides.

If flooding is used to treat snake phobias, the person is immediately given the snake to handle, with no other preceding stages. They are asked not to escape the situation but to hold the snake until their anxiety disappears. Flooding can sometimes last hours but is generally a quicker version of the treatment as there is no gradual buildup.

～

VISUALISATION AND REPETITION

Whether gradual or abrupt treatment is used, before being exposed to the fearful situation or object, the person would typically practise visualisation. This involves imagining themselves in the feared situation. While visualisation is not enough on its own —any mental rehearsal must be followed by a real and direct situation—it is an effective first step in the exposure process.

The treatment typically has to be repeated to overcome our fear completely and rewire the memory circuits of the amygdala. So, using the abrupt or gradual approach, one exposure session would not typically be enough to eliminate the fear and change the amygdala's response. It would have to be repeated until the shift has been made.[57]

WHICH TREATMENT IS BEST?

Evidence suggests that, in theory, the flooding approach — in which people are exposed to their fear in an extended and rapid way — is the more powerful and quicker method. However, for any treatment to work, people must be willing and able to do it. Therefore, anxious people often prefer the more gradual approach. While this approach may take longer, it is usually more effective as people are able to start and continue with the treatment. Just as with diet and physical exercise programmes, the most direct ways to lose weight or become physically fitter aren't always the best, as people are often unable to keep up with extreme diets or fitness regimes but give up soon after they have started.

KEY CONSIDERATIONS FOR EXPOSURE THERAPY

We need to keep the following points in mind when creating an action plan for exposure treatment:

Prepare For Pain - It should now be clear that to overcome our anxiety, we have to expose ourselves to our fears. In her 1980s aerobics videos, Jane Fonda said, 'No pain, no gain!' The most effective way to rewire our anxiety response is to excite the neurons that activate the specific neural pathway holding the memories we want to change. We need to experience the situations and stimuli that create the anxiety. This will allow us to create new neural connections and pathways, changing the amygdala's response, reducing anxiety, and altering our limiting behaviour.

Discomfort is the price of admission to a meaningful life, but the courage to take difficult actions can be made easier if they are aligned with our values. Courage is not the absence of fear. Courage is fear walking. If we're not prepared to accept pain or discomfort, we are pursuing dead people's goals. Dead people never get rejected, fail, or feel anxious. We don't want dead people to be our role models.

Be Confident You Can Complete the Plan Before You Start - Confronting our anxiety in this way is difficult. We rarely go out of our way to seek discomfort and distress, so we must consider what we are taking on before going ahead. It's essential to be confident that we can go through each action plan stage. When facing situations that threaten us, the desire to escape can sometimes be overwhelming or unbearable. If we find it too much and leave the situation before the anxiety reduces, we can strengthen the anxiety response. This will teach our amygdala that escaping an anxious situation is the best behaviour to follow in similar situations in the future. So don't leave the situation when the fear is high. Keep this in mind when designing each stage of the action plan. Make sure it is doable for you. It's essential that the outcome of the exposure is positive or neutral. Otherwise, it can be detrimental. Of course, it won't be anxiety-free, and courage will be required, but we should ensure, as much as we can, that nothing bad will happen. Although this sounds distressing, the exposure won't be distressing in every moment of the treatment. You will find your experience of anxiety changing quickly, making it easier each time.

Use the ACT Mindfulness Skills Throughout the Process - You will likely have unhelpful thoughts and uncomfortable feelings or sensations during the exposure treatment. Remember, we must defuse unhelpful thoughts, make room for uncomfortable feelings, and then engage with the present. Accept, welcome, and allow the fear to be there until it subsides.

You may also benefit from changing how you interpret fear symptoms. We talked about how important mindset is earlier in the book. Adding to that evidence is some new research suggesting that if we interpret our fear as 'excitement', we're more likely to use it to take action, resulting in more positive behaviour. This is because excitement, like fear, is a high-arousal state. Eliminating a high arousal state is almost impossible, but reinterpreting it is relatively easy. The research demonstrated that re-framing fear as excitement increased performance in many tasks, particularly those involving social evaluation.[58] So accept fear, welcome it as a friend, and use it to your benefit when possible.

Practise Exercises That Desensitise You to the Uncomfortable Physical Symptoms - If you find the physical symptoms of anxiety particularly uncomfortable, practise exercises that simulate these symptoms before you do the exposure. For example, do intense physical activity to accustom you to a racing heart. Spin around in a circle to simulate dizziness and lightheadedness. This will allow you to become familiar with these feelings and sensations, making it easier to accept and handle them in threatening situations.

Repetition is Your Friend - The more we repeat our exposure to the feared situations, the more we activate the specific circuitry and the stronger the new pathway gets. Both gradual and abrupt exposure require repeated behaviour. For example, if you fear walking down a busy street in front of others, walk down multiple busy streets in different areas, on different days, and at various times.

Choose Your Battles Carefully - We should use exposure in the situations that impact our lives most, and only when necessary. It's reasonable to withdraw from a situation or avoid it altogether if the anxiety doesn't present much of a problem or has little consequence for us. If you don't enjoy riding large roller coasters and it overwhelms you with fear, it won't hold you back in life if you never bother to ride them. If you are afraid of public speaking but have no desire to speak in public and are never required to do so, then the fear won't impact your life. However, when our anxiety is holding us back from doing something we value or want to do or causes us extreme distress and arises frequently, then we need to work on tackling and overcoming it.

Avoid Using Safety Behaviours - In Chapter 3, we made a list of the 'hiding behaviours' we often use to minimise our anxious symptoms. These behaviours vary between individuals, but common ones include using smartphones, tablets or sunglasses as props to hide behind, sticking with a safe person at a social event, and arriving early at social gatherings to avoid interacting with others. Safety behaviours in exposure treatment can lead to partial results and are often far less effective.

DESIGNING THE EXPOSURE TREATMENT PLAN

All exposure treatment plans are individual, as the experience of social anxiety differs from person to person. Only you will know the specifics of your social anxiety. Professional help with designing exposure treatment is beneficial, but this option won't be accessible to everyone. If you're unable to create a plan with a therapist or medical professional, carefully use the following steps. It shouldn't be rushed or done on impulse, as an inappropriate plan can worsen anxiety. In the next chapter, after you've designed your exposure treatment plan, we'll embed it into a safe structure to make it as beneficial and effective as possible.

· · ·

1. Select the Social Situation You Want to Focus on

First, you need to decide which area of your social anxiety to focus on. Remember, focus on the situations that most impact your life. The ones that are holding you back from properly living. The situation should be specific and relate closely to your real-life experiences. For example, fear of going to a shop to make a purchase will differ depending on the type of shop (small corner store or department store), type of purchase (new clothes or bottle of water), type of environment (hometown or unfamiliar city), etc.

2. Choose the Type of Exposure Treatment

Next, you must decide whether to 'jump in the deep end' with flooding or use the more gradual, 'easy goes it' approach of systematic desensitisation. The gradual approach should be a step-by-step plan that sees you working up to the most challenging part of the social situation over time. The abrupt flooding approach involves you starting with the most challenging part of the situation. We'll make a plan for the gradual approach, but if you want to use flooding, begin at the most challenging point.

3. Create an Exposure Hierarchy

Creating an exposure hierarchy involves breaking down the challenging social situation into a list of steps in rank order, starting with those that cause the least anxiety and progressing to the most challenging. When you begin the exposure treatment, you will go through the steps one by one in sequential order.

i) Find the Extremes

We start creating this list of steps by first identifying the components of the social situation that provoke the most and least anxiety. We use these two components as the extremes and then identify at least five steps in the middle. For example, a person who fears going into a cafe for a drink may say that the most stressful part of the situation is talking to the person behind the counter, and the least anxiety-provoking part of the process is walking along the street towards the cafe.

ii) List the Intermediate Components

Now, we need to list the challenging components that fall into the middle of the two extremes. The list of challenging intermediate components in our example may include:

- Deciding what to order.
- Waiting in line with other customers to be served.
- The physical sensations typically experienced in public places due to anxiety.
- Being stared at by other customers in the cafe.
- Selecting a table to sit at and walking towards it.

iii) Order the components From Least to Most Threatening

Next, we make a numbered list, sorting the components of the challenging situation from least to most threatening by rating them between 1 and 100, where 1 = not at all anxious and 100 = highest possible anxiety.

1. Walking in the street towards the cafe (10).
2. Being stared at by other customers in the cafe (25).
3. Deciding what to order (30).
4. Waiting in line with other customers to be served (40).
5. Selecting a table to sit at and walking towards it (55).
6. The physical sensations typically experienced in public places due to the anxiety (70).
7. Talking to the person behind the counter to order a drink (90).

iv) Accomplish Each Step

The goal of the exposure therapy is now to complete each step until the anxiety reduces. In our example, this means walking on the street towards the cafe several times before going to the next step. This can be done over a period of time. When using the gradual method, you don't have to complete all the steps immediately. It's important to remember that you must stay in the situation until your anxiety reduces, or you could make the anxiety worse. If you rated the anxiety level of a step as 70, I'd suggest that you make sure that the anxiety has fallen to at least half of that (35) before you leave the situation. Your amygdala needs to learn by experience that escape isn't necessary, that these situations will not harm you, and need not initiate the fight-or-flight response.

Use the ACT mindfulness skills of defusion, expansion, and engagement to help you cope with anxiety. Each step should be done repeatedly. The more anxious you feel about the step, the more practice you need. It usually gets easier with each repetition, but as we don't have control over every situation, this may not always be the case. There will be ups and downs, but this should not throw you off course. Overall, the experience will get better.

Now that we understand how to design an exposure treatment plan, we will embed this plan into a safe and effective structure in the next chapter.

FIFTEEN

The Social Anxiety Action Plan

The dress rehearsal is now over. It's time to take action. It's easy to read through a book like this, try a few exercises, but then put it down and get distracted by responsibilities, chores, tasks, and work. Getting started is vital.

This may seem scary, but it will be up to you to set the pace. Don't be afraid to start small. Sometimes, the goals we automatically select, without thinking, are so great that we cannot possibly do them, or at least not in the timeframe we imagine. We get discouraged before we've even started. This is because massive change feels overwhelming. Let go of the idea that you will change your entire life all at once, but understand that you can take action using small incremental steps.

The Social Anxiety Action Plan aims to help you move out of your comfort zone, tackle some of the small challenges you face, and begin to take action and change your behaviour. Even if these changes seem minor. Beginning with small, manageable behaviours will also allow you to gain momentum, build confidence, create self-belief, and develop a growth mindset, nurturing the belief that you can change your behaviour and how you respond to anxiety.

The plan outlined in this chapter embeds the exposure treatment into a structure that makes it as effective and safe as possible. It involves choosing a social situation, creating an intention, practising mental rehearsal, simulating physical symptoms, completing the steps of the exposure treatment, and then repeating the process with a new social situation. Let's look at this more closely.

Exercise: The Social Anxiety Action Plan

A template for this exercise can also be downloaded here: http://bit.ly/2ripJpj

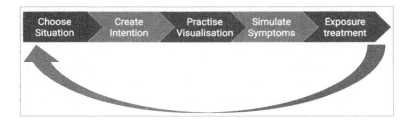

1. CHOOSE THE SOCIAL SITUATION: The first step is choosing a social situation you want to tackle. As we've already discussed, starting small may be beneficial so you don't immediately get overwhelmed. Remember, only choose the situations that most impact your life, the ones holding you back from living.

Social Situation:	

2. CREATE AN INTENTION: By raising awareness of how we think we are perceived and setting an intention to change this, we can dramatically change the way other people see us. This includes strangers, friends, and acquaintances. With small changes and consistent behaviour, it's never too late to change how others view you. Creating an intention has three stages: writing two brief paragraphs and one further short sentence. The writing part of the exercise is essential; just thinking it through won't produce the same results.

Stage 1: Write a paragraph describing what you believe is the first impression you currently make in your chosen situation. How do you usually 'show up' in this situation, and how does that cause other people to perceive you? Think about how you talk, your body language, and your expectations of the situation.

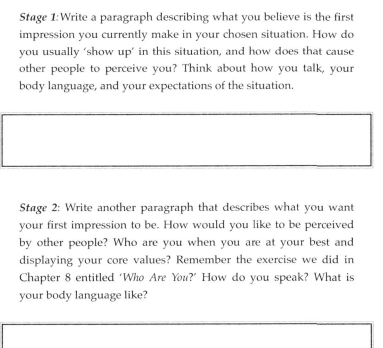

Stage 2: Write another paragraph that describes what you want your first impression to be. How would you like to be perceived by other people? Who are you when you are at your best and displaying your core values? Remember the exercise we did in Chapter 8 entitled '*Who Are You*?' How do you speak? What is your body language like?

Stage 3: Write a short statement describing what you project to others today and what you will project to others tomorrow. For example, I might write, *"Today I am shy and timid, but tomorrow I will be more curious and engaging"*. This is called the intentional first impression. The intentions we set for ourselves can considerably impact our behaviour. Whenever we create an intention, we subtly form or reinforce a mental habit. If we consistently create the same intention, it will become a habit guiding our behaviour. Intentions can shape our behaviours, days, and lives.

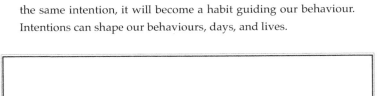

3. PRACTISE VISUALISATION: Visualisation is sometimes called imagery, mental rehearsal, or mental practice. It refers to the creating or recreating of an experience in the mind. The process involves constructing or recalling from memory pieces of information stored from experience and shaping these pieces into meaningful images. It is like playing a film in your mind of the social situation you intend to undertake. As an example of visualisation, a tennis player might use visualisation by mentally rehearsing their serve in detail before playing a match or visualising a previously effective and winning performance before going on the court.

MRI scans have indicated the brain doesn't distinguish between an imagined or actual experience, so preparing for a challenge using visualisation can be a valuable tool before stepping out and practically applying exposure treatment. Imagining the detailed process of the steps you'll be taking has many benefits. As we said, the brain can't tell the difference between a real and an imagined experience, so going through a challenging task in detail can be excellent preparation.

Welsh rugby union player Leigh Halfpenny often prepared for his goal-kicking by visualising the process in his hotel room before the game. He would imagine the crowd, the tension, various kicking distances and angles, going through every single motion he would do for a real kick.[59] I would often do the same before important talks or lectures I had to deliver that I was anxious about (not as glamorous as kicking the winning points for Wales, I know). If possible, I would go to the room of the talk some hours, days, or weeks beforehand to see the exact environment. I'd imagine how it would feel full of people. If I couldn't access the room or hall, I'd try to find photos of it online. I'd often check how the street and building looked on Google Maps before interviews or talks and imagine walking into the building in preparation.

Visualising challenges in this way can also prepare us for mistakes or things going wrong. Sticking to sporting analogies, the Olympic record-holding swimmer Michael Phelps often used mental rehearsal in this way. He visualised his goggles filling with water, a competitor doing better than expected, or losing count of his strokes, and would then go through the process of how he would react, training himself to think clearly under pressure. His visualised scenarios sometimes came true, and as he had already rehearsed them in his mind, he could deal with them calmly and effectively.[60] We can use this same technique in social contexts, from public speaking to job interviews to difficult conversations.

Try to add to the visualisation in as many practical ways as possible. If you must wear formal clothes for a talk or social gathering, visualise and practise wearing formal clothes. Students taking one of the courses I teach have to do their assessed presentations in formal suits, so I would always allow them to book time in the room that would be used for the assessment. I also encouraged them to dress in the clothes they would wear on the day of the presentation, both when practising at home and the venue. Try to make the visualisations as accurate as possible. Practise visualising each step of the exposure treatment at least three times.

Visualisation Practise	Score quality of this session out of 10
1	/10
2	/10
3	/10

4. SIMULATE THE PHYSICAL SYMPTOMS: As mentioned in the previous chapter, if you find the physical symptoms of anxiety particularly uncomfortable, practise exercises that simulate these symptoms before you do the exposure (intense physical activity to raise heart rate, etc.). You only need to complete this step if physical symptoms are a particular problem for you, so feel free to skip this step if you're confident that the physical side of anxiety isn't an issue in your case.

Exercise	Symptom Simulating
E.g. running	E.g. Raised heart rate
1.	
2.	
3.	
4.	
5.	

5. COMPLETE THE EXPOSURE TREATMENT: Now, go through the steps of the exposure treatment plan you designed using the information you completed in the 'Designing the Exposure Treatment Plan' section (see previous chapter).

Stage 1 – Situation:

| |
| |

Stage 2 - Type of Exposure Treatment (Gradual or Abrupt)

_____

Stage 3 - Create an Exposure Hierarchy

a) Find extremes

Component with least anxiety	
Component with most anxiety	

b) List intermediate components

	Intermediate Components
1	
2	
3	
4	
5	

c) Order all components from least to most threatening and rate each component out of 100 (where 1 = minimum anxiety and 100 = maximum anxiety.

	Component	Rating (/100)
1	(component with least anxiety)	
2		
3		
4		
5		
6		
7	(component with most anxiety)	

d) Complete each component step-by-step. Write down each component stage in order and keep a note of how many times you have completed the stage.

	Component Stage	Times Completed
1		
2		
3		
4		
5		
6		
7		

After you have completed the first step, you move on to the next exposure treatment step and so on, until you have completed all the steps. You should find that the exercise will become easier as you progress through the steps, and your confidence will grow.

The actions of confidence come first. The feelings of confidence come second.

HELP! I'M STUCK!: TROUBLESHOOTING THE SOCIAL ANXIETY ACTION PLAN

What if you feel stuck and unable to complete one, some, or all of the stages of the exposure treatment? What holds us back from doing something we'd like to do or doing uncomfortable things we don't like but need to do, often making a situation much worse? There are three common reasons, and we've discussed these reasons before.

- **1. Fusing with our thoughts**: The mind hooks us with thoughts and stories, and we get lost in them. These thoughts aren't a problem when we're defused from them, but when we fuse with them, they become obstacles.
- **Antidote:** Defusion. Next time you're stuck, ask yourself, 'What am I fusing with?' You can notice it, name it and neutralise it using one of the defusion exercises outlined in Chapter 8, and then engage fully in what you are doing.

- **2. Excessive goals**: We will fail if a goal exceeds our resources. So ask yourself if you're trying to do too much too soon. It's good to dream big, but you must be realistic to avoid getting discouraged.
- **Antidote**: If you're having problems with the initial goals of your exposure treatment, try to start with a smaller goal. If you have already tried smaller goals and are stuck on the next one, try to break the exposure treatment down into even smaller steps. So, instead of having seven steps (two extreme components and five intermediate

components), create ten steps or more. This may help break down the social situation into smaller, more manageable behaviours. Remember, tortoise, not hare.

- **3. Avoiding discomfort**: You feel discomfort when you step outside your comfort zone. If you wait for your discomfort to go or don't make room for it, you may wait a long time. Ask yourself, what thoughts and feelings am I trying to avoid or get rid of?
- **Antidote**: Accept discomfort. Are you willing to make room for the discomfort when you step outside your comfort zone? Difficult emotions and sensations will arise. Growing and exploring new horizons may bring many fears, but the alternative is stagnation and personal cost. Accepting the discomfort will also bring a new sense of meaning, purpose, and personal growth.

So, getting unstuck will involve defusion, expansion, engagement, overcoming your fear, and possibly breaking your exposure treatment into even smaller steps.

My final request is that you start to apply the exercises practically. It will take courage and persistence, but it can be done. Remember, change is possible. Embrace a mindset that allows you to believe this. Nothing will change if you only read the book. You must take action.

The next part of the book is an extra section that focuses on emergency exercises and will be helpful for those who suffer from extreme symptoms of anxiety and stress. These are helpful for all types of anxiety situations, including social interactions and gatherings.

PART V
Emergency Exercises

MANAGING FIGHT, FLIGHT, OR FREEZE

SEVENTEEN

Calming the Anxiety Response

Throughout the book, we've discussed what anxiety is, how it develops, when it is useful, and when it becomes a problem. Most of the strategies centre on exercises that change our relationship with social anxiety, helping us manage our anxious thoughts, uncomfortable feelings, and resultant behaviours. We've focused on not allowing anxiety to keep us stuck, hold us back, or stop us from living a meaningful life.

However, what if we're particularly panicked, anxious, angry, or stressed and need help immediately? Maybe we feel trapped in a situation: sitting at an exam, feeling overwhelmed, panicking before a job interview, feeling faint when waiting for a medical appointment, or waking in the middle of the night to a feeling of dread.

This section contains short and simple exercises that focus on reducing the physiological symptoms of anxiety. You won't be surprised to learn these exercises help us switch from the sympathetic nervous system, which we should all know by now is very aggressive, to the parasympathetic nervous system, which is much calmer.

We described the role the amygdala plays in anxiety in Chapter 5. We said it is involved in both routes and is the part of the brain that initiates the emergency arousal system: the fight, flight or freeze response. Once the challenge or emergency response has kicked in, whether through the thought-based cortex route telling the amygdala to react or directly through the reactive route of the amygdala itself, our ability to think and respond to the anxiety reaction logically is limited. So, recognising the arousal response and understanding what is about to happen before it occurs or just after it starts is vital to responding to it appropriately and reducing anxiety quickly.

Once the emergency response is up and running, the chances of thinking our way out of it are limited. Indeed, our cortex can misinterpret why these symptoms occur and convince us that something dangerous is happening or will happen. This can heighten our anxiety response further, and we can become trapped in a negative feedback loop.

Remember, when our emergency arousal system is activated, the sympathetic nervous system is energised, releasing stress hormones such as cortisol and adrenaline. This produces rapid physiological responses, including increased heart rate, elevated blood pressure, rapid breathing, blood flowing to the extremities, slowed digestion, and increased sweating. This response is beneficial when we're in danger, providing extra strength and alertness. This gives us a better chance to escape more swiftly, fight more powerfully, or freeze and hide away more effectively.

This happens within a fraction of a second before we consciously know what is happening. It's wired this way to help save our lives, so it can't be based on higher thinking; there is no time to ponder strategies of how and best to react. It's a vital, life-saving, hard-wired system that we need when in genuine danger. However, it's not so helpful when we respond this way when presenting in front of an audience, noticing our neighbour's car parked on our grass, or opening a letter from our bank telling us our account is overdrawn.

So, when we are experiencing the physiological symptoms of anxiety triggered by the fight, flight or freeze response, we need to be aware of this and target the amygdala directly. We will look at two different categories of the physiological anxiety response and suggest exercises that can help both—firstly, the aggressive **fight-or-flight response** and then the **freeze response** to anxiety.

FIGHT OR FLIGHT EXERCISES

The following exercises are intentionally short and simple. Remember, they are designed to help you switch quickly from a defensive and aggressive state to a much calmer one. These exercises should be practised if you're feeling particularly panicked, anxious, angry, or stressed and don't want to behave or feel that way. As with all the other exercises in the book, the more you practise them, the quicker they will work and the more effective they will be. Read through the exercises, try each out, and then pick one or two that work best for you and use them when needed.

Fight or Flight Exercise 1: Three Deep Breaths

This exercise is quick and effective. By slowing down breathing and taking deep breaths, we can direct our body from the sympathetic system's stress response to the parasympathetic system's relaxation response.

Step 1: Take a short, strong, gentle, inward breath through your nose for two seconds, then breathe slowly out through your mouth for 5-7 seconds.

Step 2: Repeat step 1 another two or three times. The response is almost immediate and surprisingly powerful. If you find you're still experiencing powerful physical anxiety symptoms, try to breathe normally for about a minute and then repeat the exercise.

Fight or Flight Exercise 2: Nostril Breathing

Nostril breathing has been proven to activate the parasympathetic nervous system, reduce blood pressure, and enhance respiratory functions. The instructions may look complicated initially, but you'll realise it's a simple exercise once you've completed the steps. You can find a video of the exercise here: http://bit.ly/2rExWr0

Step 1: Sit in any comfortable seated position. Relax the body and breathe naturally for a few moments, allowing your mind and body to settle.

Step 2: Rest your left hand on your lap or knee. Make a 'peace sign' with your right hand. Rest the two extended fingers lightly on the bridge of your nose. Place your thumb gently onto your right nostril. Place your ring and little fingers gently onto your left nostril.

Step 3: Close your eyes and begin by softly closing your right nostril (using your right thumb). Then, inhale slowly, deeply, smoothly, gently, and without strain through your left nostril.

Step 4: Close your left nostril (using your ring and little fingers) and release the closure of your right. Exhale through your right nostril. Inhale through your right nostril.

Step 5: Close your right nostril and release the closure of your left. Exhale through your left nostril.

This completes one round. You can continue the pattern from steps 3-5 for as long as you wish. When you're finished, relax both arms, sit, and breathe naturally for a few moments before opening your eyes.

Fight or Flight Exercise 3: Getting Present

This exercise is designed to bring you into the present moment and out of thoughts and feelings of panic:

Step 1: Sounds: For one minute, notice what sounds you can hear in the surrounding environment. Rather than striving to hear sounds, allow the sounds to come to you. Each time your attention wanders away from the sounds and back to your thinking, gently and with compassion, bring it back to the sounds.

Step 2: Objects: For one minute, notice up to three objects you can see in your environment in as great detail as possible (shape, colour, texture, etc.). Imagine you are a visitor from another planet and have never seen these objects. Each time your attention wanders away from the objects and back to your thinking, gently and with compassion, bring your attention back to the object.

Step 3: Now, try to engage in the present moment and focus on what is happening in your immediate environment.

Fight or Flight Exercise 4: The Pause

This exercise is useful when we feel like we are losing control of our emotions, particularly when we're getting lost in our reaction to a person, situation, or event. This exercise calms the amygdala and gives us greater access to our prefrontal cortex, enabling us to act more calmly and effectively.

The Angry Sergeant

Before outlining the steps, I'll summarise a true story told by

Tara Brach, a psychologist and meditation teacher, that illustrates the power and effectiveness of the exercise.[61]

She describes how a Sergeant in the United States Army called into a supermarket on his way home from a mindfulness-based anger management course. He was rushing to get home and got very irritated as he stood waiting in a queue to pay for his groceries. A woman before him was holding a baby, waiting to pay for only a few items. The Sergeant thought the woman should have gone to one of the express checkouts without clogging up his queue. To make matters worse, when the woman was being served, she handed the baby to the cashier, and they chatted for a while. He felt his irritation and anger growing but then remembered one exercise from his anger management course.

He paused and then asked himself what was happening inside his head at that moment; he tried to be aware of the story playing in his mind and observe what he was thinking and feeling. He noticed anger, and underneath the anger, he noticed anxiety about being late, and underneath the anxiety, he became aware of a fear of losing control. He stayed with this anger and discomfort for a while and found a little space. In that small gap of awareness he had created, he noticed how lovely the baby was and how much the two women enjoyed her.

When he got to the front of the queue, he remarked to the cashier that the baby was adorable. "Oh, thank you." The cashier said, "Actually, that's my little girl. My husband was killed in Afghanistan last year, so my mother brings her by a few times a day so we have a little time together."

This illustrates that if we sometimes don't pause and deepen our attention, we can find ourselves constantly caught up in the stories in our heads, living out patterns that separate us from our best selves and others and often make difficult situations worse.

An audio version of this exercise can be found here:
https://soundcloud.com/dr-matt-lewis/the-pause-mp3

Step 1: Pause. Stop for a moment. Breathe. Notice your breathing for 10 to 20 seconds.

Step 2: Notice what is going on inside your mind and body. What stories are you telling yourself? What emotions are there? What is happening in your body? Observe your thoughts and emotions and look for some space. Are you tense? Notice how your body feels.

Step 3: Now, bring your attention to the present moment. What is happening around you in your environment? What can you see and hear? Try to engage with what is happening around you without judging.

Fight or Flight Exercise 5: The Bell Hand

This exercise involves focusing on your dominant hand while opening and closing it. It's an effective exercise for focusing your attention away from unhelpful thoughts and on to the present moment, activating the calming parasympathetic nervous system.

The movement involves softening the palm by drawing the fingers inward towards it, but neither closing the hand into a fist nor totally stretching out the palm and fingers. Instead, the focus is on the gentle opening and closing movement of the fingers and softening of the palm, which can be coordinated with breathing.

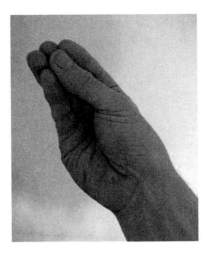

Step 1: Start with the palm of your dominant hand open and flat. Exhale and slowly and gently draw your fingers and thumb inward whilst keeping them straight (so you're not making a fist) until your fingers and thumb meet. See the photo below. Focus your attention intently on the movement and how it feels.

Step 2: Then, as you inhale, slowly open your hand again. Repeat this until you start to feel calm. If your attention wanders away, gently bring it back to focusing on the movements of your hand.

Fight or Flight Exercise 6: Focus on the Soles of Your Feet

You can do this exercise standing or sitting down. If sitting on a chair, adjust your spine to be straight but not rigid. Your eyes can be open or shut (eyes shut is best, but if you're not able to do this as you're not in private, keep your eyes open and lower your gaze).

Focus on the Feet

Focus your attention on the sensation of your feet on the ground. Notice the exact sensations: the weight, temperature, tingling, the feeling of your shoes, or nothing at all if that is the case. Notice when your mind takes over with its commentary, and as soon as it does, note where it took you and then bring your focus back to your feet. Keep bringing your attention back to your feet until about two minutes have gone by.

～

Fight or Flight Exercise 7: R.A.I.N

We can use the acronym R.A.I.N. to help us find a little space when dealing with difficult emotions.

Step 1: **Recognition**: When feeling overwhelmed, it's difficult to think clearly; it feels as if your head is full of red mist. Firstly, recognise whatever you can within the swirling mist, such as anxiety, fear, rage or sadness. Identifying an emotion means you're regulating it and using your prefrontal cortex to calm the aroused limbic system.

Step 2: **Acceptance**: All emotions are okay. The harm is done in the way you think about them. Whatever the feeling is, it is just a feeling; you don't have to act on it. Let it pass through because, in the next second, it will change, anyway. Let go of the shame and blame; they will never get you anywhere other than back to being locked into unhelpful thinking.

Step 3: **Investigation**: Focus your attention on wherever the emotional pain is in your body. As soon as you tune into the sensation in your body, the story inside your head changes. Investigate inside: Is your chest tight? Is your stomach churning? Is your jaw clenched? If you register nothing, that's fine, too.

Step 4: Non-Identification: Step away from the emotions and give them space, knowing this will pass, too. Stop the struggle. With this distancing, you're developing self-regulation, reducing the intensity. You're focusing on the raw sensations rather than the thoughts behind them and the 'whys' and 'wherefores'. You won't immediately snap out of your anger, anxiety, or stress, but you will give yourself a small gap, enabling you to reflect in the midst of it all. The more you practise, the faster you get at identifying and exploring your emotions.

THE FREEZE RESPONSE

When discussing the fight, flight, or freeze response, the 'freeze' part of the arousal system is often overlooked. If the brain assesses, accurately or not, fighting or fleeing the situation is not an option, or the traumatic threat is ongoing, the limbic system can simultaneously activate the parasympathetic nervous system (the more calm state), causing a state of freezing called 'tonic immobility' – like a deer caught in the headlights, or a rabbit playing dead when spotted by a hunting dog. This can happen in situations in which you don't have enough hormone-assisted strength or speed to respond to an overwhelming emergency by fighting or running away.

When this happens, we can sometimes dissociate from being in the present moment. This can help us not to feel the overwhelming enormity of what is happening. Hormones, including endorphins, can be released, acting as an analgesic and reducing the pain of mental or physical injuries. Additionally, if you're not putting up a fight or running away, the person or animal attacking you might lose interest in continuing their attack. If you can't make the attacker stop by fighting or fleeing, the brain thinks it is better to disappear within itself and block out what is too overwhelming and frightening to take in.

As with the fight-or-flight response, the freeze response can also be triggered in relatively safe situations. Some people seem more prone to the freeze response and are more likely to be withdrawn rather than experience feelings of panic. However, research has indicated if we use an active coping strategy when we feel frozen, withdrawn, and immobilised like this, we can undo the freeze response and train our brains to respond in this way in similar situations in the future.[62]

Freeze Response Exercise: Do Something Active

This exercise may seem simple, but starting in the middle of a freeze response can be difficult. Research suggests you should find something active you can do when you feel frozen. Almost anything active: do a jigsaw puzzle, tidy up, or call someone on the phone. Social activities can be particularly helpful when feeling frozen. Indeed, anything that involves pleasurable interactions with others. The key is to do something that interrupts the freeze response of the amygdala.

Often, when experiencing the freeze response, people feel too anxious to do anything. They may stay in bed and avoid work or other commitments. However, by shifting the amygdala to a more active response, they find the interruption creates some momentum and allows them to engage in activities that may have seemed overwhelming beforehand.

Plan Ahead

It can be challenging to think of something active to do while in the middle of a freeze response, so plan ahead. When you are functioning well and feel in control, think of activities you could easily do and that are readily available, and make a list. Then, when you feel immobile, it will be easier to choose something active without thinking too much about it. Try to raise your awareness of experiencing the freeze response, notice when it is happening, and then take action.

EIGHTEEN

Dealing with Panic Attacks

P anic attacks can last from anywhere between thirty seconds to thirty minutes and can be so distressing sufferers sometimes feel they are losing control or about to die. The experience can be one of extreme agitation, terror, fury, or immobilisation, accompanied by extreme symptoms of the fight, flight or freeze response: racing heart, rapid breathing, trembling, shaking, nausea, numbness, tight chest, difficulty swallowing, and hot flushes or chills. Episodes can return in waves, are frightening and often exhausting.

The attacks are typically initiated when the amygdala responds to a trigger in the environment that the person may or may not even be aware of. They can be triggered by situations, smells, sounds, or feelings based on deeply held fears or associational memories. They can often occur at inappropriate times and are due to an overreaction by the amygdala, often in response to a cue or trigger that doesn't pose any real threat or danger. The physiological responses would be appropriate and helpful in the case of a real threat or an emergency.

Most people will experience some sort of panic attack once or twice in their lives. Those who have more regular panic attacks can start to fear them, and this anxiety can become a self-fulfilling prophecy, with an attack being triggered simply by the fear of having one. For example, a person may once have had a panic attack at the cinema, so during their next visit to the cinema, they fear the same thing happening again, which can trigger panic attack symptoms. This can lead to the person avoiding the cinema altogether and then avoiding other public places in the future. This is the *Escape Avoidance Learning* we discussed in Chapter 6, and it can lead to agoraphobia and other clinical anxiety disorders.

Important: Don't Escape the Situation!

When suffering from a panic attack, it's vital that you resist the strong impulse to escape the situation. Although panic attacks are very frightening and uncomfortable, they can't physically hurt you. Fleeing from the situation may make you feel better in the short term, but in the long term, it will reinforce the power of the attacks and make it more challenging to overcome them.

We discussed earlier in the book that the amygdala learns from experience. So, staying in the situation will help the amygdala learn that it is safe and that it need not react in the same way in the future. While this is much easier said than done, it would be beneficial to see these situations as opportunities to work on changing the anxiety response, reducing and eventually eliminating further episodes.

Although it is challenging to calm a panic attack through logical thinking, there are some things you can do during an attack that will help reduce the ability of the cortex to create the conditions in which the panic attack can get worse:

1. **Understand it's only a feeling**: Interpreting the symptoms of a panic attack as life-threatening can cause the symptoms to worsen. So it's essential to recognise you are having a panic attack and nothing more. This will ensure you don't add fuel to the flames.

2. **Don't worry about what other people think**: In the middle of a panic attack, people often feel embarrassed and worried that others are judging them. Don't let your cortex try to predict what other people think. It is probably wrong anyway and will only add to the stress and panic.

3. **Don't focus on the panic attack**: Try not to obsess about when a panic attack may come. Not worrying about panic attacks is one of the best ways to avoid them. Constantly focusing on bodily sensations like sweating and butterflies in the stomach can lead you to think yourself into a panic. While again, this is easier said than done, if you find yourself thinking or worrying about a possible panic attack, use one of the defusion exercises in Chapter 11 and then focus your attention on the present moment. With practice, these defusion techniques will become easier and work faster.

So what should we do if we recognise symptoms of a panic attack starting or suddenly become aware we're caught up in one? How can we best cope? While we can't immediately stop the attack, a number of strategies can reduce the power of the symptoms and shorten the duration of the attack. These strategies help us switch from the aggressive sympathetic nervous system to the calmer parasympathetic nervous system.

Always remember that you must avoid escaping the situation to eliminate or significantly reduce future panic attacks. This can be difficult at first and will require patience and courage, but with time and practice, it will get easier. Experiencing short-term fear will provide you with long-term peace.

Panic Attack Exercise 1: Deep Abdominal Breathing

An audio version of this exercise can be found here:
    https://soundcloud.com/dr-matt-lewis/calming-panic-attacks-audio-exercise

Deep breathing can be effective when having a panic attack, as many of the symptoms we experience are related to hyperventilation, which is fast and shallow breathing. When we go into hyperventilation, we breathe out carbon dioxide too quickly, resulting in low levels in the body. This is identified immediately by the amygdala and triggers a highly reactive response. This is why people experiencing a panic attack are advised to breathe into a paper bag; the bag will capture the expelled carbon dioxide, allowing it to be inhaled back into the bloodstream. However, by using conscious deep breathing, we can relax the amygdala and prevent hyperventilation or bring it under control after it has been triggered.

Step 1: Sit as comfortably as you can, placing one hand on the chest and one on the stomach. If you cannot sit down, you can still do this exercise standing up.

Take a deep breath in and see which part of your body rises. People often find that their chest rises as they breathe in. However, effective abdominal breathing will cause your stomach to expand as you inhale and retract as you exhale. Your chest shouldn't move much at all.

Step 2: Try to focus on breathing deeply, expanding your stomach as you fill your lungs with air. You should feel your stomach rising underneath your hand when you breathe in. Many people tend to pull their stomachs in as they inhale, which keeps the diaphragm from expanding downward effectively. So focus your attention on your stomach rising as you inhale.

Important Note - Some people find focusing on breathing increases their anxiety, especially if they have asthma or other conditions that cause breathing difficulties. Use the other recommended exercises if you find the breathing exercises uncomfortable.

Panic Attack Exercise 2: Progressive Muscle Relaxation

An audio version of this exercise can be found here:

https://soundcloud.com/dr-matt-lewis/progressive-muscle-relaxation-pmr

A panic attack often results in muscle tension throughout the body, and tight muscles also tend to increase amygdala activation. So, learning and practising muscle relaxation techniques will help shorten panic attacks and make them less likely. If you are prone to panic attacks, you should practise the following exercise regularly so you can use it quickly and effectively when experiencing severe anxiety.

The exercise uses a two-step process. First, you systematically tense particular muscle groups in your body. Then, you release the tension and notice how your muscles feel when you relax them. Anxious people are often so tense throughout the day that they may not recognise what being physically relaxed feels like. Through practice, you can learn to distinguish between the feelings of a tense muscle and a completely relaxed muscle.

Then, you can begin to initiate this relaxed state quickly at the first sign of the muscle tension that accompanies your feelings of anxiety. By tensing and releasing, you learn what relaxation feels like and how to recognise when you are tense.

When first trying the exercise, it should take around 10-15 minutes to complete. You can also practise with different muscle groups for 2-3 minutes at a time. You don't have to be anxious when you practice it. Practising it when you are calm can make it easier to do when feeling anxious or panicky.

Step 1: Getting ready: If possible, find a quiet, comfortable place to sit, close your eyes and let your body go loose. You can lie down, but this will increase your chances of falling asleep. Although relaxing before bed can improve your sleep, the goal of this exercise is to learn to relax while awake. Take between three and five slow, deep breaths before you begin.

Step 2: Apply muscle tension to a specific part of the body: Focus on a specific muscle group, such as your left hand. Take a slow, deep breath and squeeze the muscles as hard as possible for about 5 seconds. It is essential to feel the tension in the muscles, which may even cause a bit of discomfort or shaking. In this instance, you would make a tight fist with your left hand. It is easy to tense other surrounding muscles accidentally (for example, the shoulder or arm), so try only to tense the muscles you are targeting. Isolating muscle groups gets easier with practice.

Step 3: Relaxing the tense muscles: After about 5 seconds, let all the tightness leave the tensed muscles. Breathe out as you do this step. You should feel the muscles become loose and limp as the tension flows out. Deliberately focus on and notice the difference between tension and relaxation. This is the crucial part of exercise. Remain in this relaxed state for about 10 seconds and then move on to the next muscle group.

Step 4: Repeat the tension-relaxation steps with the other muscle groups: To make it easier to remember, you can start with your feet and systematically move up (or if you prefer, do it in the reverse order, from your forehead down to your feet).

For example:

- Foot (curl your toes downward)
- Lower leg and foot (tighten your calf muscle by pulling toes towards you)
- Entire leg (squeeze thigh muscles while doing above)

(Repeat on the other side of the body)

- Hand (clench your fist)
- Entire right arm (tighten your biceps by drawing your forearm up towards your shoulder and 'make a muscle' while clenching your fist)

(Repeat on the other side of the body)

- Buttocks (tighten by pulling your buttocks together)
- Abdomen (suck your stomach in)
- Chest (tighten by taking a deep breath)
- Neck and shoulders (raise your shoulders to touch your ears)
- Mouth (open your mouth wide enough to stretch the hinges of your jaw)
- Eyes (clench your eyelids tightly shut)
- Forehead (raise your eyebrows as far as you can)

Step 5: Relax: After completing all the muscle groups, take one minute to enjoy the state of relaxation.

Learning to relax the body and notice the difference between tension and relaxation can take time. At first, focusing on your body can feel uncomfortable, but it can become enjoyable over time.

Panic Attack Exercise 3: Quick Tense and Relax

Once familiar with Exercise 2, you can practise a short version of progressive muscle relaxation. In this approach, you learn how to tense larger groups of muscles, which takes even less time. These muscle groups are:

1. Lower limbs (feet and legs)
2. Stomach and chest
3. Arms, shoulders, and neck
4. Face

So, instead of working with just one specific muscle at a time (e.g., your stomach), you can focus on the complete group (your abdomen and chest). You can start by focusing on your breathing during the tension and relaxation.

When doing this shortened version, it can be helpful to say a particular word or phrase to yourself as you slowly exhale (such as "relax," "let go," "stay calm," or "peace"). This word or phrase will become associated with a relaxed state; eventually, saying this word alone can bring a calm feeling. This can be beneficial during times when it would be hard to take the time to go through all the steps of progressive muscle relaxation.

Panic Attack Exercise 4: Release Only

You can further shorten the time you take to relax your muscles by becoming familiar with the 'release only' technique. One benefit of tensing and releasing muscles is learning to recognise what tense and relaxed muscles feel like.

Once you are comfortable with this, you can do 'release only', which involves removing the 'tension' step of the exercise. For example, try just relaxing the muscles instead of tensing your stomach and chest before relaxing them. At first, the feeling of relaxation might feel less intense than when you tensed the muscles beforehand, but with practice, the release-only technique can be just as relaxing.

Remember, practising progressive muscle relaxation is often vital, whether you're anxious or not. This will make the exercise more effective when you need it. It may seem a little tedious at first, but it can become a very effective tool for treating anxiety and reducing the power and duration of panic attacks.

Panic Attack Exercise 5: Physical Exercise

If you're in a place where you can move about when having a panic attack, it would be very beneficial to pace or exercise. Remember, this is the emergency arousal system kicking in, preparing your body to fight or flee, so physical exertion is what your body is ready to do. If your sympathetic nervous system is activated, you can use it as nature intended. If you run or walk briskly when anxious, you'll use the muscles prepared for action. Exercising will also burn off excess adrenaline and use the glucose released into the bloodstream by the stress response.

Many physical sensations you experience when exercising are similar to how the body reacts when the emergency arousal system has been activated: increased heart rate and blood pressure and faster breathing. So exercising can also be a form of exposure therapy, allowing you to experience and get used to these physical changes, making us less afraid and more accepting of the sensations over time.

PART VI
Resources

_____

AUDIO EXERCISES AND EXERCISE TEMPLATES

Appendix 1: Online Resources

CONTACT DETAILS

www.DrMattLewis.com

If you have enjoyed this book, I would be very grateful if you would leave a review on Amazon.

AUDIO EXERCISES

All audio exercises and meditations can be found at:

https://soundcloud.com/dr-matt-lewis

EXERCISE TEMPLATES

Safety Mode Exercise 1: The Costs of Avoidance:
http://bit.ly/2rqEg25

Safety Mode Exercise 2: The Costs of Hiding Behaviours:
http://bit.ly/2rZUK4F

Preparing to Change Exercise 1: Who Are You?:
http://bit.ly/2rY7BCm

Preparing to Change Exercise 2: Balancing Life:
http://bit.ly/2qHFo1y

The Social Anxiety Action Plan:
http://bit.ly/2ripJpj

ONLINE COURSE

The original online course can be found here:
https://www.udemy.com/course/overcome-anxiety/

OTHER BOOKS

Overcome Anxiety: A Self Help Toolkit for Anxiety Relief and Panic Attacks contains some replica information from this book, but extra exercises and a focus on general anxiety.

U.K. Link: http://amzn.to/2rZtfsl
U.S.A Link: http://amzn.to/2siMgqk

Appendix 2: Medicating Anxiety

ONLINE BONUS CHAPTER

Medicating Anxiety: Should I take Anxiety Pills? Pros, Cons, Side Effects, and Consequences

This chapter can be found online by using the following link: https://goo.gl/3H92Io

Notes

1. Lewis, M. (2016). Overcome Anxiety: A Self Help Toolkit for Anxiety Relief and Panic Attacks. Createspace, U.S.A.

2. Nieto, S.J., Patriquin, M.A., Nielsen, D.A. and Kosten, T.A. (2016). Don't worry; be informed about the epigenetics of anxiety. Pharmacology Biochemistry and Behavior, 146-147, pp. 60-72.

3. Ito, T.A., Larsen, J.T., Smith, N.K. and Cacioppo, J.T. (1998). Negative Information Weighs More Heavily on the Brain: The Negativity Bias in Evaluative Categorizations. Journal of Personality and Social Psychology, 75 (4), pp. 887-900.

4. McLeod, S. A. (2010). Stress, Illness and the Immune System. Retrieved from www.simplypsychology.org/stress-immune.html

5. Draganski, B., Gaser, C., Busch, V., Schuierer, G., Bogdahn, U. and May, A. (2005). Neuroplasticity: Changes in grey matter induced by training. NeuroReport, 16 (17), pp. 1893–1897.

6. Pittman, C.M. and Karle, E.M. (2015). Rewire Your Anxious Brain: How to Use the Neuroscience of Fear to

End Anxiety, Panic and Worry. New Harbinger Publications, Oakland, pp. 38.

7. Harris, R. (2008). The Happiness Trap. Robinson, London, U.K.

8. Boyd, T.L. and Levis, D.J. (1983). Exposure is a necessary condition for fear-reduction: A reply to De Silva and Rachman. Behaviour Research and Therapy, 21 (2), pp. 143-149.

9. McGonigal, K. (2015). The Upside of Stress: Why Stress is Good for You (and How to Get Good at It). Vermilion, London, U.K.

10. Crum, A.J. and Langer, E.J. (2007). Mind-set matters: exercise and the placebo effect. Psychological Science, 18 (2), pp. 165-171.

11. Crum, A.J., Corbin, W.R., Brownell, K.D. and Salovey, P. (2011). Mind over milkshakes: mindsets, not just nutrients, determine ghrelin response. Health Psychology, 30 (4), pp. 424-129.

12. Crum, A. J., Akinola, M., Martin, A., & Fath, S. (2017). The role of stress mindset in shaping cognitive, emotional, and physiological responses to challenging and threatening stress. Anxiety, Stress, & Coping, 30(4), 379–395. https://doi.org/10.1080/10615806.2016.1275585

13. Boudarene, M., Legros, J.J. and Timsit-Berthier, (2001). Study of the stress response: role of anxiety, cortisol, and DHEAs. L'Encephale, 28 (2), pp. 139-146.

14. McGonigal, K. (2015). The Upside of Stress: Why Stress is Good for You (and How to Get Good at It). Vermilion, London, U.K., pp. 28-32

15. Cocking, C. (2016). Brussels terror attack victims show how humans help each other in times of crisis. [ONLINE] Available at: https://theconversation.com/brussels-terror-attack-victims-show-how-humans-

help-each-other-in-times-of-crisis-56707. [Accessed 17 June 2016].

16. Strecher, V.J. (2016). Life on Purpose: How Living for What Matters Most Changes Everything. HarperOne, U.S.A., pp. 19-34.

17. Strecher, V.J. (2016). Life on Purpose: How Living for What Matters Most Changes Everything. HarperOne, U.S.A., pp. 35-99.

18. Dickerson, S.S. and Kemeny, M.E. (2004). Acute stressors and cortisol responses: a theoretical integration and synthesis of laboratory research. Psychological Bulletin, 130, 355-391.

19. Pip, S. (2015). Jon Ronson Part 1. Distraction Pieces Podcast with Scroobius Pip. N.p., 2015. Web. 22 June 2016.

20. Mauss, I.B., Savino, N.S., Anderson, C.L., Weisbuch, M., Tamir, M. and Laudenslager, M.L. (2012). The pursuit of happiness can be lonely. Emotion, 12(5), pp. 908-912.

21. Salmela-Aro, K. and Nurmi J.K. (1996). Depressive symptoms and personal project appraisals: A cross-lagged longitudinal study. Personality and Individual Differences, 21 (3), PP. 373-381.

22. Trew, J.L. and Alden, L.E. (2015). Kindness reduces avoidance goals in socially anxious individuals. Motivation and Emotion, 39(6), PP. 892-907.

23. Gilovich, T., Medvec, V.H. and Savitsky, K. (2000). The spotlight effect in social judgment: An egocentric bias in estimates of the salience of one's own actions and appearance. Journal of Personality and Social Psychology, 78(2), pp. 211-222.

24. Williams, M. and Penman, D. (2011). Mindfulness: A Practical Guide to Finding Peace in a Frantic World. Hachette, London, U.K., pp. 211-216.

25. Taylor, W.F. (2010). The Principles of Scientific Management. Cosimo Classics: New York, U.S.A.

26. Dijksterhuis, A.P., Bos, M.W., Nordgren, L.F. and van
    Baaren, R.B. (2006). On making the right choice: The
    deliberation-without-attention effect. In: Newport, C.
    (2016). Deep Work: Rules for Focused Success in a
    Distracted World. Piatkus, London, U.K., pp. 144-145.

27. Berman, M.G., Jonides, J. and Kaplan, S. (2008). The
    cognitive benefits of interacting with nature.
    Psychological Science, 19 (12), pp. 1207-1212.

28. Berman, M.G. (2012). Berman on the Brain: How to
    Boost Your Focus. [ONLINE] Available at:
    http://www.huffingtonpost.ca/marc-
    berman/attention-restoration-theory-
    nature_b_1242261.html [Accessed 20 June 2016].

29. Newport, C. (2016). Deep Work: Rules for Focused
    Success in a Distracted World. Piatkus, London, U.K.,
    pp. 149-150.

30. Rizzolatti, G. and Craighero, L. (2004). The mirror-
    neuron system. Annual Review of Neuroscience, 27 (1),
    pp. 169–192.

31. Kouider, S., Andrillon, T., Barbosa, L.S., Goupil, L. and
    Bekinschtein, T.A. (2014). Current Biology, 24 (18), pp.
    2208-2214.

32. Van der Helm, E., Yao, J., Dutt, S., Rao, V., Saletin, J. M.,
    and Walker, M. P. (2011). REM Sleep Depotentiates
    Amygdala Activity to Previous Emotional Experiences.
    Current Biology : CB, 21(23), 2029–2032. http://doi.
    org/10.1016/j.cub.2011.10.052

33. Changa, A.M., Aeschbacha, D., Duffy J.F., and Czeislera,
    C.A. (2014). Evening use of light-emitting eReaders
    negatively affects sleep, circadian timing, and next-
    morning alertness. Proceedings of the National
    Academy of Sciences, 112(4). DOI:
    10.1073/pnas.1418490112

34. Burkeman, O. (2016). Shuffle your thoughts and sleep.
    [ONLINE] Available at: https://www.theguardian.

com/lifeandstyle /2016/jul/15/shuffle-thoughts-sleep-oliver-burkeman. [Accessed 29 July 2016].

35. Lee, I., et al. (2012). Effect of physical inactivity on major non-communicable diseases worldwide: an analysis of burden of disease and life expectancy. Lancet, 380, pp. 219-229.

36. Ratey, J.J. (2010). Spark!: The Revolutionary New Science of Exercise and the Brain. Quercus, London.

37. DeBoer, L. B., Powers, M. B., Utschig, A. C., Otto, M. W. and Smits, J. A. (2012). Exploring exercise as an avenue for the treatment of anxiety disorders. Expert Review of Neurotherapeutics, 12(8), pp. 1011–1022. http://doi.org/10.1586/ern.12.73

38. Johnsgard, K. W. (2004). Conquering Depression and Anxiety Through Exercise. Prometheus Books, Amherst, NY.

39. Broocks A., Meyer, T., Gleiter, C.H., Hillmer-Vogel, U., George, A., Bartmann, U. and Bandelow B. (2001). Effect of aerobic exercise on behavioral and neuroendocrine responses to meta-chlorophenylpiperazine and to ipsapirone in untrained healthy subjects. Psychopharmacology, 155 (3), pp. 234-241.

40. Heisler, L.K., Zhou, L., Bajwa, P., Hsu, J. and Tecott L.H. (2007). Serotonin 5-HT(2C) receptors regulate anxiety-like behavior. Genes Brain Behavior, 6 (5), pp. 491-496.

41. Biddle, S.J.H., Mutrie, N. and Gorely, T. (2015). Psychology of Physical Activity: Determinants, Well-Being and Interventions. Routledge, U.K., pp. 96-119.

42. Ratey, J.J. (2010). Spark!: The Revolutionary New Science of Exercise and the Brain. Quercus, London, pp. 85-112.

43. Broman-Fulks, J.J. and Storey, K.M. (2008). Evaluation of a brief aerobic exercise intervention for high anxiety sensitivity. Anxiety, Stress & Coping, 21 (2), pp. 117-128.

44. Williams, S.E., Carroll, D., Veldhuijzen van Zanten, J.J.C.S. and Ginty, A.T. (2016). Anxiety symptom interpretation: A potential mechanism explaining the cardiorespiratory fitness–anxiety relationship. Journal of Affective Disorders, 193, pp. 151-156.

45. Barton, J., Bragg, R., Wood, C. and Pretty, J. (2016). Green Exercise: Linking Nature, Health and Well-being. Routledge: U.K.

46. Gerbner, G., Gross, L. Morgan, M. and Signorielli. N. (1980). The "Mainstreaming" of America: Violence Profile No. 11. Journal of Communication. 30 (3), pp. 10-29.

47. Pinker, S. (2012). The Better Angels of Our Nature: A History of Violence and Humanity. Penguin: London, U.K.

48. The Fallen. Retrieved from http://www.fallen.io/ww2/

49. Siegel, D.J. (2007). The Mindful Brain (Reflection and Attunement in the Cultivation of Well-being). W. W. Norton & Company, New York, U.S.A., pp. 66-69.

50. Gerber, P., Schlaffke, L., Heba, S., Greenlee, M.W., Schultz T. and Schmidt-Wilcke T. (2014). Juggling revisited - a voxel-based morphometry study with expert jugglers. Neuroimage, 15 (95), pp. 320-325.

51. Treadway, M.T. and Lazar, S. (2008). The Neurobiology of Mindfulness. In Germer,C.K., Siegel, R.D. and Fulton, P.R. (2013). Mindfulness and Psychotherapy. 2nd ed. New York: Guilford Press, pp. 183

52. Gard,T., Hölzel, B.K. and Lazar, S.W. (2014). The potential effects of meditation on age-related cognitive decline: a systematic review. Annals of the New York Academy of Sciences, 1307, pp. 89–103. http://doi.org/10.1111/nyas.12348

53. Davidson, R.J. and Begley, S. (2012). The Emotional Life of your Brain: How Its Unique Patterns Affect the Way

You Think, Feel, and Live – and How You Can Change Them. Hudson Street Press, New York, N.Y.

54. Jerath, R., Barnes, V.A., Dillard-Wright, D., Jerath, S. and Hamilton, B. (2012). Dynamic change of awareness during meditation techniques: neural and physiological correlates. Frontiers in Human Science, pp. 6, 1-4.

55. Lazar, S.W., Kerr, C.E., Wasserman, R.H., Gray, J.R., Greve, D.N., Treadway, M.T., McGarvey M., Quinn B.T., Dusek J.A., Benson H., Rauch S.L., Moore C.I. and Fischl,B. (2005). Meditation Experience Is Associated with Increased Cortical Thickness. NeuroReport, 16 (17), pp. 1893–1897.

56. Wolitzky-Taylor, K.B., Horowitz, J.D. , Powers, M.B. and Telch, M.J. (2008). Psychological Approaches in the Treatment of Specific Phobias: A Meta-analysis. Clinical Psychology Review, 28, pp. 1021-1037.

57. Pittman, C.M. and Karle, E.M. (2015). Rewire Your Anxious Brain: How to Use the Neuroscience of Fear to End Anxiety, Panic and Worry. New Harbinger Publications, Oakland, pp. 134.

58. Brooks, A. W. (2014). Get excited: Reappraising pre-performance anxiety as excitement. Journal of Experimental Psychology: General, 143, pp. 1144– 1158.

59. Campbell, A. (2015). Winners and How They Succeed. Penguin Random House, U.K., pp. 206-207.

60. Campbell, A. (2015). Winners and How They Succeed. Penguin Random House, U.K., pp. 203-204.

61. Ferriss, T. (2015). Tara Brach On Overcoming Challenges And The Fear Of Missing Out. The Tim Ferriss Podcast. N.p., 2015. Web. 7 June 2016.

62. LeDoux, J. E., and J. M. Gorman. (2001). A Call to Action: Overcoming Anxiety Through Active Coping. American Journal of Psychiatry, 158, pp. 1953–1955.

Printed in Great Britain
by Amazon

47680848R00116